If Streetlights Glow Ultraviolet

Thoughts from a Scottish Highland Year of Autism Positives

Katherine Highland

ISBN: 978-0-244-09205-4

Author's Notes

An earlier version of this book was printed and sold in house by Autism Initiatives in 2015. It contained a selection of these thoughts with each one expanded upon. It was produced in A4 size and had colour illustrations. These have been changed to black and white for this published version to keep costs down.

This book contains additional material. The thoughts themselves are numbered, to make the index compatible with both paperback and Kindle versions; paragraphs which do not start with a number are the notes I added to expand upon them.

I am deeply grateful to Autism Initiatives for their support with the original concept and printing, and to David and Gwen Morrison at PublishNation for their help getting this book into wider circulation after working with me on my coping strategies book, Deferred Sunlight, which was written after this one and published before it!

Contents

Introduction

This book came from a personal project which was to write down a positive thought, experience or memory to do with autism, every day from 18th June 2013 to 18th June 2014. As well as being Autistic Pride Day, 18th June is a special day for me. It was the date of a big planning meeting in 2012 during the ongoing work to establish the Highland One Stop Shop, based in Inverness but providing a service for autistic adults widely throughout the Highlands. I came to this long fought battle very late on, eventually fulfilling my dream of moving from Edinburgh to the Highlands to be part of it. I lived first in Aviemore and later in Nairn, travelling to Inverness and volunteering as well as being the first service user to register. Many autistic people and dedicated professionals had been working together for several years to try to make a long term service happen; I saw many of them at that June 2012 meeting. I had arrived on the scene with a lot to learn; despite my inauspicious debut, those people accepted me and that meeting stood out as the culmination of this acceptance.

The idea to make something of my personal celebration of that anniversary which would benefit the one stop shop came to me on the Highland Chieftain, the daily train which runs between Inverness and London King's Cross. That train is central to my life as you will see in this book! I came up with the idea of the positive thoughts for a year and inviting others to contribute, then decided I would make a booklet out of them to be used as a fundraiser. The service was still new when I did the challenge so there were only a few guest contributions; those which did not end up in the book were all my own. I have added some new notes and updates for the 2018 publication but the thoughts themselves are all from that 2013-2014 project.

About Katherine Highland

I was born in July 1972 and diagnosed autistic in January 2008. I was still living in Edinburgh at the time and had ended up in trouble at work through lacking the strength and self knowledge to handle an ongoing bad situation appropriately. I was left with severely worsened mental health. I write under a pseudonym as my family is unaware of any of this. I will always be grateful to Jane Watt, my cognitive behavioural therapist, for seeing the possibility of my being autistic and broaching the subject sensitively, helping me to open my eyes and come to terms with it; to appreciate it as a positive as well as explaining a lot of the negative. I am equally grateful to Andrew McKechanie, the specialist registrar from the Lothians diagnostic service who assessed me with the utmost respect, consideration and empathy. This led me to Autism Initiatives and Number 6. I don't have enough words to express how much they have done for me; Stewart and Andy in particular, helping me to understand my past and present and prepare better for my future, respecting my contribution and enjoying my sense of humour!

Then the new chapter finally opened as I moved up here and became part of the Highland One Stop Shop (HOSS). When I left Edinburgh, I spent a few nights at the Royal Highland Hotel in Inverness to have a break and celebrate before everything was delivered to my new home. Chatting with other guests in that much loved and always supportive environment, when I told them of my love for the Highlands, having dreamed of moving here for nearly 25 years and my chance to be involved with developing services for autistic adults one of them said I should write a book about it. I never forgot that; the year of positives idea gave me the framework to make it happen.

1: I went to a local restaurant where I am a known regular customer and usually order one of three items. Today I wanted something different as it was better suited to what I would be having later at home. The waiter said he bet I was going to order one of my three usuals. I resisted the compulsion to do so or to explain; just ordered and let it be the good-natured laugh moment it was.

It is so easy to lose sight of the moments in life which are simply a bit of fun; the lighter side of a serious, complex world. We analyse so much and have a need for precision. That's fair enough; that's autism and it has its benefits. We pay attention to the fine details and often keep other people right! Sometimes, though, we need to remind ourselves that not everything has multiple layers of meaning; not every social situation is a trap. For our own sakes, sometimes we need to remember just to be.

2: Voluntary work I do in the office at the Strathspey Railway can be stressful as it is often busy, noisy and people are coming in and out. After several difficult sessions in a row, I felt apprehensive but today was quieter and so much fun. Someone had saved a spreadsheet as "Coach booing sheet" instead of "booking" by mistake and my colleagues and I were in fits imagining standing in the car park booing at the buses.

It is important to notice and hold on to these small, fun moments when we are doing activities which push our limits. They help us to remember our motivation and keep going when we are finding the activities difficult.

3: A brown envelope from the DWP came today and I thought it may be the start of the dreaded reassessment.

In fact it was good news; they owed me some backdated benefit. Much as that made my day, however, the real warm glow staying with me is the knowledge that if it had been bad news, moral support, backup and practical help would have been just a phone call, text or email away at the HOSS.

A certain community spirit has grown around the dread of the brown envelopes containing letters from the official department which deals with disability benefits. Regular reviews cause a lot of worry and distress. Some people have taken to posting on social media when, for instance, there is a cold weather payment due in a particular area so that others will know to expect one of these brown envelopes and know that chances are it is not one of the scary ones. I love the solidarity this demonstrates.

4: Celebrated the summer solstice at the HOSS today, drinking 7-Up out of plastic champagne flutes with the team and some of the service users. Lots of laughter and shared experiences of the far North and the rural Highlands. Felt a connection out from the city.

I've always loved the bright city lights and needed to live where there is easy access to amenities since I don't drive. At the same time, I am very much aware of the small rural communities within the area covered by the HOSS but a long way from Inverness, how hard the people there have to push for equal access to services and the responsibility we have to be accessible to them without them having the added burden of having to fight for it. At the summer solstice I often recall a dark, cold early evening at the opposite end of the annual cycle of seasons when I stood in the station looking at the departures board and became fascinated by the names on the Far North line to Wick and Thurso. Forsinard, Altnabreac, Scotscalder, Georgemas;

they looked so evocative and called to me. The illuminated dot matrix style of the lettering on the dark background of the board picked out each name as a cluster of points of light in the blackness, the configuration of each forming the unique pattern identifying each place. To me that was a miniature representation of just what those far off places are; each individual cluster of lights out there way up in the winter blackness of the Flow Country into which the evening Caithness-bound train would be heading. That moment became an idea and then a plan for a visit in the summer to walk from Forsinard to Altnabreac. I love the contrast between the lightest and darkest times of year; how each seems so far off and mysterious from the viewpoint of the other.

5: Reading a BBC News Online article about the decipherment of an ancient language known as Linear B, I was fascinated by the potentially autistic traits (though autism was not mentioned) in the two scientists to whom the article referred; solitude, obsessive and meticulous life's work, possible communication / social barriers. Imagining them never understanding themselves was a poignant reminder of how lucky we are to have diagnosis and a growing service. I also loved the tantalising final reference to a mysterious Linear A!

It often saddens me, and many other autistic people, to think of the struggle faced by the unknowing multitudes of us who lived before autism was discovered as a diagnosis and a way of being. How much of what could have been a better quality of life never came to be; how much talent and contribution stayed locked away in a misunderstood, unsupported life. So many lost the potential for fulfilment and a personal context in which every achievement could be deservedly enjoyed to the full. As an adopted Highlander with my love of the place intensified by my autistic emotions, I wonder how many of the people who had to cope with being sent away during the Clearances had their anguish intensified by a condition they never knew they had; never given an answer as to why others in the same situation appeared to cope better with the change and loss. It breaks my heart to think of it; at the same time it makes me extra thankful for the HOSS and the era in which we live now.

6: The soothing opaque orange streetlights around where I live are being replaced by very bright white ones; this is a difficult change as I love it when the streetlights are on and loved the orange ones and though I also love white ones as they are like moonlight, these ones are too bright. However, seeing them on in heavy rain for the first time was a revelation; like watching a hypnotic shower of diamonds.

I have always loved streetlights; some might say it is one of my special interests, though I am becoming slightly sceptical about the tendency to describe it as a special interest every time an autistic person speaks enthusiastically about something! When I was a child, the streetlights were the first thing I noticed whenever I was taken somewhere new and I couldn't wait to see what colour the light was when they came on at dusk. I love that they are set out to an ordered pattern yet can look random as though someone had grabbed a handful of sparkling jewels and scattered them. I often use them as a subject in photography.

Burnside, Aviemore

7: Being given some contact details (as part of my work with the HOSS) for transitional support based in high schools in the region felt very encouraging, knowing that in the modern era of cyberbullying and increased lifestyle related pressures, there is a positive side in increased support and understanding for young autistic people and our own service base helps to get awareness of that support increased.

Bullying remains a blight on our society, affecting all vulnerable groups including a high proportion of autistic people throughout all stages of life. With our self doubt heightened by a lifetime of miscommunications and lack of understanding why things went wrong, especially for people diagnosed in adulthood, we can be very vulnerable to gaslighting (having problems deliberately created or worsened by others who then claim we are imagining it). So often the bullies have been bullied themselves and are in fact very low, unhappy people inside; a system which does not protect people from being bullied is failing the bullies too as some of them could be turned around with a bit of guidance and support if caught early enough. Being bullied can have the effect of building character but even for the strongest, most resilient autistic person, especially in childhood, it can be a disproportionately long road. As a child I never understood why trying to be a good sport didn't make my peers change their minds and accept me, as it went in the school stories I read. Communication and consistency are key to support and resolution.

8: Watching a programme about night buses in London, one driver was describing how he loves the night shift as it really allows him to appreciate the architecture of the city while the streets are less crowded. It was so refreshing to see this kind of perspective; looking in a different way at something many people dislike, i.e working nights. Being autistic often affords similar creative thinking.

Hearing about others' perspectives on what brings them pleasure from less obvious sources is so interesting. This is the kind of thing of which autistic people are sometimes stereotypically thought to be unaware!

July 2013

9: (Contributed by a guest): I was out for a walk when I saw a young woman whose pose and behaviour suggested she may have been contemplating suicide. I asked her if she were OK and after speaking with her for a long time, I asked if she had any family or a partner who could help. She explained that she had a boyfriend who was very kind but did not know how she felt. I suggested she tell him and offered to see her home. She did not want to be accompanied but I believe that I gave her hope. I feel that my knowledge of my autism gave me the right balance of empathy and detachment to offer support in a practical, non judgmental and impartial way.

This is a major achievement by one of my fellow service users who did not want a fuss made but told this story as an illustration of how autism can work the opposite way to what many people imagine. Far from being about lack of connection or empathy for others, it increases sensitivity to what is happening around us, to a degree which can be unbearable. It is processing these unexpected events and the general input from the outside world which can be so problematic and sometimes make us shut down. Although we will never know what was in that young woman's mind nor what happened afterwards, his highly commendable actions prove how much we can achieve when we can find the courage to take that step into the unknown upon seeing that someone could be in danger and need help.

Staying objective and listening without judgement was a vital skill in such a scenario; knowing when his role in resolving it was completed and moving on, an advanced social awareness.

10: Sometimes two strands of life which haven't been going so well can both turn for the better at the same time, which is very powerful. Met an elderly neighbour who hadn't spoken to me for a while as she knows I love cats and had blamed me for them coming into her garden; spoke to her as I have continued to do and she stopped for a pleasant chat. Then a tourist asked us for directions, which is something I have a fear of as my mind goes blank but the two of us made a successful team and helped.

I dread being asked for directions; almost two decades living in Edinburgh gave me plenty of practice at finding ways to cope with it but the words "Excuse me" still invoke a reaction of fear. In the Highlands, the next words are often "Are you local?", to which even after more than two years up here I still respond with a triumphant "Yeeeeeeeeeessssssssss!" However, that still doesn't mean I will necessarily know or be able to effectively recall and set out the direction they need and I cannot bear to disappoint or annoy people. As soon as I am asked, I feel responsible for seeing it through and if I cannot give them an answer I feel very guilty. It is hard to let go of that sense of responsibility and it can overshadow the rest of the day. So when my neighbour was there to back me up, it was a bonus; even without the other circumstances, it was a treat not to have to deal with it on my own for once. Incidentally, I am now very close to the neighbour mentioned and have kept in touch with her since moving away. Helping her out through harsh winters and a serious illness made any past misunderstandings melt away and enriched both our lives.

11: Despite frustration at being tired all day due to a medication change coinciding with a heatwave, I am reclaiming the night hours I love; outwith conventional routine, sitting out with a decaffeinated coffee in the garden with the soothing glow of the streetlights and nobody around! Treated my garden table and chairs with oil so that they can be kept outside all night and they were dry before a bird deposited on them; an everyday miracle!

The unpredictability of the British weather, especially up here in the Scottish Highlands, creates an expectation throughout society that people must go outside as much as possible when the sun's out. It can feel almost like a crime not to go out if we are free to do so on a sunny day! I do like the sunshine and I do enjoy getting out but feeling that it is compulsory can take a lot of joy out of it. Sensory issues also make it more difficult to cope with hot temperatures. Sweating, clinging clothes and glare, both direct from the sun and reflecting off surfaces even when wearing dark glasses, can all be intensely uncomfortable. Places will inevitably be more crowded as people make the most of fine days. Some medication increases skin sensitivity and risk of sunburn. Of course it can be annoying when I mean to go out but take longer than expected to do everything I need to or become so engrossed in what I am doing that I don't manage it. I am coming to accept that it is perfectly allowable to sometimes enjoy the sun streaming in through my windows and spend the day doing whatever it is I need to do.

12: Just coming to the end of a few days in Inverness to spend time with friends who are up from Edinburgh. Have been enjoying the creative randomness of conversations in the HOSS, about musical notes, colours and Lord of the Rings. Loving the opportunity to listen and learn from others' own interests such as these, as well as mine (trains etc) being so genuinely accepted.

A vital part of what the HOSS environment facilitates is giving autistic people the incentive and security to let go of a bit of pressure. Even just being able to release some of the sense of urgency to get it right socially helps in a world which often marginalises us both intentionally and unknowingly. Many of us spent years before diagnosis trying to figure out why we were struggling so badly and when we managed, why it seemed to take so much more out of us than it did others.

13: Reminiscing with some railway friends today about a time when I lived in Edinburgh and after a stressful day at work I went to Waverley Station to touch base with my true life. The Orient Express was in on a tour and despite no make-up, bad hair day and feeling tired and drab, I got on and had a look inside. Our dream world can sometimes be unexpectedly close.

I have always felt at home around the railway. As a woman, I admit to getting a certain pleasure out of bucking the "trains as a male autistic interest" stereotype in my own way! In modern times, everyone has had to get used to the dynamics on the railway needing to change. Security is more of an issue than it used to be and enthusiasts are no longer so free to mingle, film and take photographs in major stations. This has been a very hard adjustment for many and the potential for shock and distress to autistic people is clear. We do tend to be rule followers and when we are suddenly told not to do something when we have been freely doing it for a long time, enjoying it and cherishing it as one of the good things we can rely on, it can be a devastating blow. We absolutely do sometimes miss a shift in the boundaries of a familiar context; an unexpected, subjectively hostile change can lead us to react in ways which are interpreted as challenging. At the same time, railway staff and police doing their safety critical work do not necessarily have all the information they need to appreciate the effect this has had on the person they needed to advise. I have seen online footage of some confrontations which I found very upsetting to watch; there was no claim that they involved autistic people but I am sure that in many instances they did. As ever, communication and accessible advocacy is the way to reduce these unfortunate incidents and lead to greater autism acceptance. The way to achieve this is to seek the input of autistic people; to give us the time and variety of communication methods we need to give that input, and to listen, believe and accept it when we do.

14: Seeing Andy Murray win the title at Wimbledon thereby banishing forever the looming spectre of being known for never quite making it made me think how important each battle won in daily life is. Victory breeds victory as the contextual pressures are lessened and confidence is boosted. When autistic in a society which is fraught with inaccessibility, the small, attainable victories are as important as any world title.

It is very important not to allow our small personal victories to be diminished by comparison to others or by subsequent bad times. Once won, they can never be taken away, even if they are a one-off.

15: Have managed a few tasks this week which are daunting for various reasons; not done before, not done for a long time or done recently and not come easily, which is the worst for me with my perfectionism and sense of being constantly on the alert / cannot afford to show any vulnerability. Had so much encouragement and sense of being cheered on from the HOSS.

We should all take into account just how exhausting and demanding it is to cope with the sense of being constantly on red alert which often goes along with being autistic. As it is with us all the time, we can lose sight of just how hard our brains are having to work. This is one of the reasons why autistic community and access to informed support is so important. Often when we are struggling more than usual it takes someone in the know but just detached enough to have a different perspective to recognise it in us and help us to share or release some of that impossibly heavy load.

16: Went out for coffee and did a lot of thinking as allowing myself to break the routine of being reluctant to spend the money on products I have at home already made me feel so much better. I came to realise I am not spending £2 on a cup of coffee; I am spending it on putting a bit of variety into my day, fighting the tendency to be isolated and giving myself more to say thereby building on the social foundation of having the HOSS.

A vicious circle can develop when social anxiety makes it difficult to go out and interact when we would like to. It means that when we are out and want to join a conversation, we struggle for things to talk about because we haven't been doing much. Even when someone needs or chooses to, for example, keep the weekends as quiet recovery time and does not intend to change that (and has every right to make that decision), the dread of the "So what have you been up to?"; "What are you up to at the weekend?" type questions adds to the difficulty when we do go out. Autistic led and proven autism accepting environments help to ease some of this burden, providing a valuable intermediate stage should we want to increase our socialising. Depending on how I feel, my genre of response may be an all-encompassing "I'll take it as it comes", a deliberately vague but still true "I don't know yet, I'm waiting to find out" (though that can lead to more questions!), or a flippant "Probably being abducted by aliens again, they didn't quite finish all the experiments last weekend!" Then again, I may have actual plans I feel I can tell people about. That always feels like a relief; that I have passed a test. It really shouldn't feel that way.

17: Enjoying a sunny day in the Highlands when I can wear shades without it making me self conscious and give my sensitive eyes a rest from the onslaught of light. It also affords a feeling of privacy; that people cannot "read" me if I do not want them to and it evens the situation if I cannot read them!

The eye contact dilemma is a big issue for many. We become exasperated by the constant correction and misinterpretation of why we don't always make eye contact in the expected way (though it is a myth that autistic people never make eye contact). It is nothing to do with being afraid or unwilling to do it. Often we are so preoccupied with our brains trying to process everything and make sense of what can and cannot be filtered out that we simply forget. There are, of course, times when indeed we would rather not make eye contact; our thoughts and feelings can be heightened and feel to us as though they must be visible to others. We are as entitled to keep them private as everyone else! I find it particularly disturbing when people have a habit of commentating on the slightest change in my facial expression or colouring. My skin flushes easily but it isn't what people understand as blushing. The slightest change in temperature can have me looking as though I embarrassed myself trying to break up a ketchup fight. It's the constant explaining that gets me. So anything that helps, whether getting a break from the pressure about eye contact by wearing sunglasses or raising awareness about the day to day reality of autism by describing these dilemmas for others to be enlightened, bring it on.

18: Really good day today. Felt like I'd been able to listen and help a lady who came in with a problem for her to understand and move forward with one thing is a huge step.

This came from an anonymous guest contributor. It is important for all of us to realise the significance of the small victories; the steps in the right direction. This applies not only to our own issues and struggles but to helping others. Because we empathise so much, we want to take all the pain away there and then. That is very rarely a realistic goal and we have to celebrate the better times within the longer process.

19: Received a 20p piece in my change which I would have trouble getting accepted as it had turned copper coloured except for one corner of silver. Felt annoyed at being seen as a soft touch and was about to complain or be spiteful and put it in the tips jar but decided to keep it as I suddenly realised it looked like a lunar eclipse, which made me feel creative instead of resentful.

It is easy to jump to conclusions and assume that people are trying to put one over on us, score points or take advantage of us having to work so hard to engage with the world. Although we are right to use caution because of our difficulties, we also need to remember that more often than not, people are just going about their day and not putting nearly as much thought into an everyday situation as we are. I smile when I remember this one as it was a small victory seeing past the instinctive mistrust to the interesting and colourful details which often elude people as we are so busy.

20: Had a good chat at the HOSS today reflecting upon friendships made there and the potential for more in the future as the service grows. It is so important that an ongoing opportunity is there as finding and nurturing new and old friendships is a long, continuing process.

So much of what the HOSS and all the one stop shops achieve in terms of improving quality of life takes time and cannot be rushed. This is why the long term security of these services is so important, so that the necessary resources can be invested. The reward and the savings to other services are immense.

21: The relief of getting a clean bill of health at the dentist and not having to go back for six months is a good reminder of the advantages of having a routine and being particular about following it. It is always nice to get a "well done; keep up the good work".

On a subsequent trip to the same dentist for my routine check-up, I will always remember the taxi journey back to the centre of Inverness. It was in the middle of a very bad bout of depression and I had really had to force myself to keep the appointment. After a conversation about dental appointments and teeth, upon dropping me off at the railway station the driver told me to keep looking after my smile. This was a genuinely lovely moment; nothing like the unwelcome heckling by strangers who shout comments like "smile" or "cheer up". The taxi driver saying that got through to me, not because it showed I had concealed my depression, but rather because it extended beyond my surface chattiness. Reaching out with a kind, genuine gesture can make a huge difference to someone who is fighting a battle we cannot see.

22: Loving that other autistic people I know appreciate and agree with my flight of fancy view that all streetlights should have an option to be switched to UV (provided harmful rays could be filtered out!) when there is snow lying, to make the most of the ultraviolet on white effect.

As well as streetlights, I love ultraviolet light. I am fascinated by the way it shimmers and softly blurs right at the edge of the visible spectrum. It marks a gateway to the unknown; the precise boundary itself a mystery, eluding perception in a tantalising haze. One of the happiest discoveries of my life was finding out that ultraviolet fairy lights actually exist and I have a set in my home.

23: The dreaded day has come when my Employment and Support Allowance review questionnaire arrived. It has been due and on my mind for a long time and has huge implications for my routine, stress levels and future peace of mind. Yet it doesn't feel as scary as I expected because the HOSS is there to back me up and give moral support.

Dealing with the benefits system is a major issue for many autistic people. Invisible conditions and the difficulties they cause, especially with regard to employment, are by their very nature unprovable and awareness of the complexities of autism is patchy at best. No two autistic people are alike and each assessment needs to be approached without preconceived ideas by the professionals involved; this puts pressure on both sides. Support for those who need to claim benefits is vital as is support for those who can do work within the limits of what our health allows. Autistic people have the reputation for black and white, all or nothing, polarised thinking but the rest of society can be just as guilty of that and more so when it comes to perceptions of benefit claiming! The importance of not having to face these processes alone and of having help to cope with the effects of the negative focus necessary for putting our case cannot be overstated. The specialised support at places such as the HOSS gives a much needed boost to morale as well as that essential perspective reminding us to take into account difficulties which have become so ingrained into our daily lives, we no longer notice them for what they are.

24: Away visiting family who are unaware of my autism because of the worry my circumstances would cause them, I am finding it a very useful reminder of how much difference it has made to my day to day life getting my diagnosis and accessing support and empathy which is waiting for me at the HOSS on my return home.

The build-up of everyday experiences which frustrate, embarrass and dishearten us can be incredibly isolating if we do not have an informed and understanding support network with which to share them. This also applies to changes which impact us intensely but would be hard for non-autistic people to understand. My move from Aviemore to Nairn took me away from the Highland Main Line, which I could see from my Aviemore home. In my autism-centred support network I found unlimited compassion and understanding for the deep sadness this caused me and the impact it had on my routine no longer having the passing trains to watch for and give structure to my day. It is amazing how much I used to get done by half past eight in the morning when it meant I could have the satisfaction of raising my first cup of coffee to the passing Highland Chieftain; the soft soothing carriage lights of the Caledonian Sleeper brought many an evening to a tranquil close. More than that, I miss them. I miss seeing and hearing them every day like I would miss any valued daily contact to which I was used. When preparing for the big day with the support of the HOSS team, I did not even have to explain why I could not face putting my model trains into a removal van. Their display cabinet could go in the van with heavy boxes and furniture around it, but not my girls themselves. Boxed and bubble wrapped in strong bags, they came with me when Gill drove me to my new home. There was so much I was spared having to explain that day: the additional sensory struggle of a typically timed heavy cold; the importance of a quiet place to eat lunch; the need to be alone for the actual moment of leaving my home of six years for the last time. Surrounded by boxes in my new home with only the bed made up and having to use the big lights (as we call the main ceiling lights in rooms in Scottish homes) while my much gentler table lamps were still packed, I had enough mental resources left over from the day to manage to go out for a meal that night. That would not have been possible without smooth, empathic support flowing throughout the day.

25: Taking a trip with family to a garden centre on a summer holiday Saturday, I took my mind off worrying about how crowded it would be by looking out for new season sensory previews; the time of deep colours, fresher air, warm spices and all the lights coming on earlier.

Distraction techniques can be very important and useful. Redirecting anxious thoughts when out and about is a satisfying thing to be able to do, just as long as we don't become so preoccupied with our thoughts that we lose awareness of surroundings and compromise our safety.

26: On the Highland Chieftain where the crews all know me, two of the staff in a row walked by my seat saying "Oh! – didn't see you there", despite my sparkly shoes, bag and clothes. This happens a lot, not just on the train and it set me thinking about what makes me so easily overlooked. I realised perhaps there is something to the theory of how we feel dictating our external image; I feel bland, therefore I am. So I need to feel more positive. Then sun and rain on the windows made my train sparkle too.

My beautiful train! The professional who first suspected and referred me for diagnosis told me that in addition to the very dark period in my life which had brought me to treatment, the intense light of my devotion to the Chieftain was a factor. At the time that terrified me as I didn't want something so precious to be seen as a medical symptom. I was also afraid that it suggested the joy that train and what I feel for the Highlands bring to my life wasn't real; that it was part of a condition. I was more resistant for that reason than for anything to do with the chaos in my life. As I learned more, I realised that this joyous aspect of my life being intensified by autism makes it more real, not less.

Dalfaber, Aviemore
(Or as I nicknamed it, Dalfabulous)
A favourite place to walk.

27: Spent a good afternoon talking with a group of fellow autistic people and it was liberating to communicate with people on such an intuitive level – and such empathy.

From a guest contributor. Many autistic people wait a long time to be able to talk with people to whom they won't need to explain about what it means to be autistic. We still have to deal with the process of getting to know one another but it is such a welcome relief not to have that additional stage to work through which can be so tiring.

28: Just had a wonderful sensory experience at today's drop-in; one of the ladies made cake AND vegetable lasagne and it was delicious!!! Oh the pleasures of being autistic and having heightened senses!!!

Another guest contribution. It is a very important point but not often emphasised that our heightened senses intensify our experience of the taste, smell and texture of food. This can be an issue when our diets become too narrow and restrictive, which is often the context in which food is mentioned in connection with autism. It is absolutely right that the serious issues around a healthy diet should be given attention. How lovely, though, to simply be reminded in an autistic context of the feelgood pleasure not only of good home cooking but of walking into that sensory experience in a convivial setting which is a safe home from home.

29: Another day when I struggled to see the funny side by the time I was making my second trip of the day, third of the week to my GP's surgery in the hope of collecting a supporting letter. Because of the time I was to call in, I had to take my recycling for the bottle banks with me and was trying to stop it making a noise; it felt inappropriate to be sitting in a doctors' waiting room with a bag of empties, but had a laugh with the receptionist, explained it was mostly from alcohol free drinks so she let me off!

Time management is a big challenge for many autistic people as we struggle with executive functioning (things like planning, making decisions, seeing tasks through to the finish despite interruptions). Although we can be very focused, fatigue and our tendency towards problems filtering out the input we actually need as our brains try to process everything around us make it difficult for us to concentrate. We can find it very exasperating when the rest of the world is not as ordered and precise as our brains want it to be, for instance when an unexpected delay or mistake means we have to allocate time for a task such as a phone call or trip to collect something all over again. It is partly our own high standards and partly the daily battle to get everything done.

30: Had a lovely message from one of the HOSS team regarding a difficult process I am going through, reminding me that they are all there for me and thinking of me. Such a warm, genuine rapport is essential to help people cope and feel they are not alone and do not have to explain autism effects on top of everything else. Much needed.

I always feel inadequate and foolish telling someone I am there for them or thinking of them as it feels so trite and lacking in any practical, measurable usefulness. It is important to remember, from my own experience, that it really can help and I should not avoid saying it just because I want to be more original and make a more quantifiable difference.

31: Coming into the HOSS after a couple of weeks away has brought a sense of coming back into the fold; it has reinforced the bonds and helped me to regain some perspective and feel less alone and worried about people.

Several people have come back to the HOSS after absences of weeks or months when they have been busy doing other things or needed time to themselves. It shows the enduring need for and value of a service like ours when people can allow their lives to take different paths knowing the service is there whenever they need it again.

32: A couple of years ago I read in the paper about a golf club vice captain taking a club member with dementia for his weekly rounds of golf and the elderly man had scored a hole in one. I kept the article on my notice board and this weekend I read that the vice captain had himself achieved a hole in one. As well as being delighted for the gentleman who deserves it for his kindness to the elderly man, it brings it home that however long the wait, our elusive goals and dream achievements should never be written off; we will have our turn.

What appealed so much about this story was the sense of a treasured routine and valued hobby combined with the added purpose of helping someone else. That is a lifestyle to aspire to.

33: Received a very favourable response to a letter I wrote to a police department raising understanding of autism after seeing an incident involving an autistic teenager on a true life TV documentary. Thanks to my feedback and information provided to me by colleagues of the HOSS for inclusion with it, autism friendly advice will be given out to the team concerned.

I had found this distressing to watch because the clearly overloaded teenager was prompted to look at the person questioning them, in a bare room with bright lights when they had pulled up their hood and lowered their head. It was known that they were autistic and there was a clear case for reaching out with some autism education. Sometimes in actual situations happening near me, I have to remind myself to question any assumptions I might be making by projecting my own feelings onto others. I once experienced an anxiety attack brought on by a stream of unwanted memories after seeing someone in a public place telling someone else to "Cheer up, it might never happen". The people involved were strangers to me; there was laughter on both sides and it was obvious they knew each other and the comment was made in mutual understanding that it was a joke. Even so, it was enough to evoke an intense reaction in me. Autistic people can have facial expressions which others read as unusual, blank, excessively serious or otherwise out of keeping with the context. Given that many of us are now being diagnosed as adults and some as elderly people, if you have never experienced this please take a moment to imagine the effect of routinely having your facial expression remarked upon, questioned and criticised right from childhood when you have no idea what is so wrong with it. Certainly in my case, by the time I was diagnosed, the damage was done. Even without these bad associations, mind you, I am strongly against anyone making the "cheer up" jibe to someone they don't know. It may be that nothing is wrong and so the person has essentially been rudely told they have a miserable-looking face, or it may be that something already has happened. The stranger who once said it to my mother when her oldest friend had just been rushed to hospital and was at that point looking unlikely to survive her illness was left in no doubt as to how ill chosen those words were. An autistic person would quite possibly freeze and have the anguish of being unable to process all of their feelings and form a response in time. How much would this add to the upset and blow to their self esteem! Every time someone thinks twice before heckling a stranger just for the sake of it, a little bit of hope is put back into the world.

34: Had a friendly text from someone I had thought was cutting me off because a change in medication is making me very low and I had said I felt taken for granted, which hadn't gone down well. Because of the support I have here at the HOSS, I have been able to step back, not get into an argument and wait, so no harm was done.

We need more alone time than many people do, yet we still yearn deeply for connection with others. Managing this paradox in our most basic needs is a very difficult one and with our tendency to perfectionism thrown in, it is desperately hard to accept that however good we think we get at balancing it, we will never be completely safe from lapses and misunderstandings. Many of my most longstanding friendships are conducted across the miles; several started out as penpals. All have very busy lives, as do I! Self reliance and self sufficiency in terms of keeping occupied and entertained are skills I have developed out of choice as well as necessity. The problem with this is, we often become a bit too good at it so that we end up with routines which our autistic rigidity then makes it difficult to vary. So although all those longings are still there, we create barriers to giving ourselves more opportunities for interaction even on our own terms. At the same time, there are occasions when people do take us for granted; good old reliable us with our set ways, always there, always duty bound to Understand for fear of further rebuke after the times when we have misjudged the boundaries! We need to be careful that we don't end up in situations where we are so afraid of being called needy (with or without justification) that we allow ourselves to be exploited by people who are aware of those fears and of what doesn't come naturally to us and use it against us. That said, it is a necessary reminder of caution but a separate issue from managing our genuine friendships. Our friends and colleagues may not always get us but this mustn't be confused with not caring or with intentionally hurting us. The most useful skills for minimising these clashes are understanding the reasons behind them, using our rigidity about rules to resolve to step back from confronting people when our emotions are running high, and discretion. It is very true that "Least said, soonest mended". This applies not only to the person by whom we feel snubbed; it includes comments to mutual friends or on social networking sites which we may regret later. I have always followed a general rule of keeping anything negative and personal off the Internet.

35: Fighting through a bad fatigue day to do some research, I was getting nowhere but kept at it and tried a few different angles. Then as it got to late afternoon, suddenly the ideas started to flow and I ended the day feeling a lot more upbeat and glad I didn't give up.

Sometimes we do need to push our limits; it is how we reach our potential and it can be good for us in the long run. There is a fine line between healthy challenge and damagingly forcing ourselves through burnout. A good support network will help us to know where that line is and identify when it has moved. The line is not fixed; it comes and goes with our health, our circumstances and age.

36: Took a long quiet walk around looking at the trees just beginning to change, the berries ripening; they are going to be wonderful this year. Felt revived enough to do some weeding in the garden when I got home. Glad my enjoyment of getting out in the fresh air and appreciating nature is restored.

Nature is a wonderful resource for us to find structure in a world full of changes. The weather may be increasingly erratic but nothing changes the way the Earth revolves around the Sun, giving us our seasons and the fluctuating proportions of daylight and dark. I find this a tremendous comfort and it makes me feel part of it all.

37: On the sleeper coming into Inverness to celebrate the anniversary of my first ever visit – 24 years ago! – with the morning turning bright and having the HOSS there on this special date for the first time, a celebratory coffee and chat to look forward to, I couldn't hold back from doing a triumphant clenched fist salute so I disguised it as a stretch, perfectly feasible in the sleeper's seated carriage even if I did only get on at Aviemore!

15th August 1989 was the best day of my life. My diagnosis was still almost two decades in my future but of course my autism was there all along and magnified every moment of the long awaited day trip. I was 17, on holiday in Perthshire with my parents and since our first holiday in Scotland the previous year I had developed an intense longing to visit Inverness. It was, and still is, a full-on autistic obsession! I had fallen in love with the place without ever having seen it, when we stood at Dunblane station on that first holiday waiting for the train to go to Glasgow for the day. The Highland Chieftain stopped at Dunblane every day in those days (only Sundays now) and was at the platform when we arrived; our train was due after. I will never know why the announcer was going against format that day but while he mentioned once that it was the London train, he announced it several times as "The train from Inverness".

I can still hear those words coming through the tannoy and echoing 25 years back in time, to the day as I write this. Yes, I wrote the original contribution on the 24th anniversary and it has worked out that I am writing this part early on the morning of the 25th anniversary before getting ready to go into the city which is now the focus of my life and work. 25 years ago on that platform, I was only vaguely aware of where Inverness was; I had no idea what it looked like, yet as I heard those words and looked up the silver line stretching out into the unknown behind the stately InterCity 125, something switched on inside me and my life truly began. A year later we had our visit there. It felt like coming home; the reality of it felt completely right. In the quarter century since then, I have had triumphs and serious lows but the absolute rightness and intense connection with my beloved Inverness never wavered.

Inverness from the Castle

38: Loving the calm of a Sunday evening with a visit to the HOSS planned for tomorrow in order to organise a very special donation of books from an invaluable colleague, friend and ally to all of us at the service. Some people are the most gracious embodiment of proof that the non-autistic world at its most complex and frighteningly nuanced can still welcome us.

A lot of people including professionals are afraid of autism because our profiles of symptoms and sensitivities are not only vastly different from person to person but can vary for each individual according to the circumstances. Fear comes as much from not wanting to get it wrong and hurt us as it comes from any preconceived idea. Then there are those who stand out for meeting us in our own world and staying on our side, working through the differences and the tough times and always asking and listening to us. We won't always agree but we treasure those who respect the journey.

39: Went out for a coffee and the waitress wanted to seat me at a typical single person's table in the corner; it was however right next to a family with two very fractious and unsettled infants. I knew I would struggle with the noise and pitch and that any objection to sitting there would be frowned upon. I got around it by choosing a small table in the other corner, "so as not to disturb the children"!

Noise sensitivity can often be at odds with how the world seems to be telling us we ought to feel. The high pitched sounds made by small children can cause actual pain, including to autistic people with children of their own. People nearby eating or coughing can also feel unbearable. There are however some noise related discomforts which just should not need to happen. Whoever manufactured a door entryphone and thought it a good idea to have the ringing sound very similar to the loud high shriek of a smoke alarm: It isn't. For so many reasons.

40: Went to my shift in the Strathspey Railway office despite being extra tired (which by my standards is saying something) after yet another very disturbed night due to medication adjustment. Ended up being treated to a tour of the inside of the visiting Royal Scotsman train; all plush purple and ornate lights, polished silver and varnished wood. Even got a paper napkin as a souvenir so I know it really happened!

Early that morning I had been emailing a friend about a high level committee of which he had recently become a member; it was autism related and went by an acronym which is also the name of a recently revived brand of whisky. I had been talking about my feelings of being overawed by this group and how it was so close by yet inaccessible to me (as a member, not as an autistic adult giving feedback, but being acquainted with about 75% of the people on it I didn't really want to have to be interacting with them as though I were a stranger). I compared it to the Royal Scotsman which visits the Strathspey Railway several times in a season but even as it sits alongside our platform it is way out of our league and out of bounds. When I was working in the office and my supervisor came in asking if I would like to be shown around the train as there were no passengers on board, it felt like a sign. As I walked towards the open door onto the observation balcony at the end of the last carriage, the angle of the sunlight made it look ethereal and dreamlike; I practically floated through the door and stood where I had always longed to get the chance to stand at the railings looking out along the track. I could hardly believe I was really there especially after what I had been writing in my email. I went on to produce the newsletter for that committee.

41: On my regular Saturday walk by the woods towards Rothiemurchus I reached the point where I usually turn back for home but a couple had just passed me and I realised it may alarm them if I appeared to turn and follow them, so to give them time to get out of range I went to look along a path which I had never investigated. It turned out to lead to a lovely peaceful spot, near enough to occupied buildings to be safe, to stand and watch the River Spey rippling over stones; very soothing.

Safety and personal security in our choice of quiet spaces and interaction, even brief, with others is something we must always prioritise.

42: Got through a day which was sad for me for reasons I couldn't really share with anyone by going out rather than sit at home and be overwhelmed by it. Caught up with some friends and colleagues at the Perth one stop shop, got some bargains in the shops, received a wonderful text message about being my own person and not needing to compete and was upgraded to First Class on the Highland Chieftain coming home.

This had to do with knowing friends of mine were representing fellow autistic people at a crucial meeting which had become inaccessible to me because of my increased social anxiety when in glamorous company which feels out of my league. My feelings of sadness and inadequacy had to be kept secret because it would have been considered internalised ableism. (Ableism is discrimination and negativity towards disabled people, viewing us as inferior rather than seeing an inaccessible society as the problem. Disabled people can also perpetrate this, especially with regard to our own limitations.) I wanted to be better at masking and "doing social" so that I could feel eligible to participate as my friends could. Reading the views of autistic and other disabled people taught me, in time, that what I should have aspired to was not to suppress my autism, hide my difficulties and earn acceptance into that project as it was, but to challenge the inaccessibility created by its ethos. Its unspoken requirement for participants to be able to network in a social setting was an accessibility issue and conflicted with its stated mission of inclusion. I don't believe this was malicious; it was more about non-disabled people working within their comfort zones without realising that was what they were doing. I did come to challenge it in my own way but because it was to do with the Highlands, I was too emotionally involved to do so pragmatically and separately from my own agenda of craving approval and belonging. Sometimes only hindsight and a bit of distance from a situation can show us what we really needed to be learning at the time. At the same time, I should have felt able to acknowledge my feelings; being sad about the loss of something or someone from our lives is legitimate and valid even if that loss arises from our disability because of ableism or inaccessibility. We are in a stronger position to challenge it constructively when we have acknowledged and properly processed our losses. It is natural and healthy to get frustrated with our difficulties at times; we can celebrate being autistic without always having to love every aspect of it!

43: In the HOSS getting ready for an open house in a few days' time as well as chasing up an overdue medical referral with the help of the staff team gave me a sense of belonging and safety on many levels. It was also lovely to see others in enjoying a chat.

Support with making phone calls is one of the many vital functions of the one stop shops. Having reduced ability to filter out ambient sound and not having the visual clues of seeing the person with whom we are speaking can make it very difficult for an autistic person to make a phone call. If we manage it ourselves because we have to, we can be left feeling exhausted and drained for the rest of the day. Writing down what we need to say can help but we cannot predict or control the other side of the conversation!

44: Walking around my home town Aviemore, which is a popular tourist destination, at the end of the school holidays gave me a sense of thrill and anticipation as the crowds will soon ease off and I will be able to enjoy being out with fewer people around. At the same time I am reminded how lucky I am to live here all year round.

In 2018, as I have already mentioned, I sadly had to move away from Aviemore. This was due to my rented house being sold and a lack of other available accommodation in the size and price range I needed. I am fortunate enough to have found a very different but still lovely, friendly and scenic new home town in Nairn, which is nearer to Inverness. It is also close enough for me to visit my friends in Aviemore frequently as well as keeping my volunteering connection open with the Strathspey Railway. Although I did not always manage to keep up my regular walks among those precious evergreens to the extent that I (and my GP) would have liked, I can at least say I never took Aviemore for granted. I was aware every day of how much I loved it and how fortunate I was. It is forever embedded in my heart.

The Harvest Moon over Aviemore

45: Set the time switches for my fairy lights now the evenings are getting darker. Really looking forward to them brightening up the house and creating a sense of festive cosiness; an ongoing celebration of living here and of the changing seasons, each with its own blessings.

Fairy lights are a wonderful sensory addition to a home, especially on a time switch to be on when we have to get up and ease us gently into the day. It is safe now that the modern ones use LEDs and don't get hot, as long as sockets are never overloaded and the plugs or transformers themselves are in a well ventilated area. The instructions that come with sets of lights will say how to use them safely.

46: My first day officially volunteering at the HOSS! That in itself felt amazing and it was so happy, warm, convivial and accepting an environment. We had visitors up from our sister services in Perth and Edinburgh, including one of my best friends. Everyone loved the place, enjoyed the day and was so excited about our Highland-wide projects.

There is a lot more to the service than what happens inside the building where it is based; we are part of a much wider community, always looking to learn from and share with the rest of our extended family.

47: Had a quiet few hours to myself today and was remembering walking home on a still January evening in Edinburgh after the meeting at which my diagnosis was confirmed. The crisp air felt full of promise as my life had started again. I took a similar walk back to my hotel in Aviemore after signing the lease on my new home here.

A winter evening walk is magical in circumstances like these, especially if there is a frost. The sparkle each tiny crystal gives off when the light hits it echoes the starbursts of awareness as a multitude of different realisations come crowding in. For my autism diagnosis, it was all the things it suddenly explained; why, for instance, I cannot filter out ambient sound to hear on the phone in a noisy environment when there's nothing wrong with my hearing itself; why at the same time I once was the only one in a crowded office to hear the alarm when a telephone handset across the room hadn't been put back right on its cradle. I knew I wasn't lying when that was quoted to challenge me as I justified not having picked up correctly what someone had said on a later occasion; I just didn't know how to explain it. For my dream move to the Highlands, it was fine details like the fact I wouldn't need to renew several years of subscriptions to the local newspapers as I would be buying them in my local shops; the memory of telling an Edinburgh friend that I wanted to be living in the Highlands by the time I was 40. Catalina has never stopped encouraging and believing; I made it with four months to spare.

48: In the midst of a bad spell of fatigue, I was feeling guilty about not having done much but a friend told me I don't realise how much I do because I just get on with things. It brought home to me how important it is that we do not become too isolated but retain the perspective of a support network such as the HOSS.

It is very important to remember and allow for the impact of fatigue on autistic people; we often don't realise how tired we are because we've never known any different. It is an area in which more understanding is needed. Everything is amplified except for our mental and physical energy. No wonder we sometimes struggle to keep up.

49: The 150th anniversary of the opening of the Highland Main Line from Perth to Inverness via Carrbridge, as we know the route today, became a day of so many positives it is impossible to pick just one, which in itself is a huge positive. Bought lots of sparkly clothes in charity shops, enjoyed sunlit train journeys and chats and laughs with random strangers. Felt alive.

Having to convince a generally inaccessible society of our needs can make us afraid to have a good day in case we undermine our case for support and reasonable adjustments. This is desperately unhealthy and needs to change. It is so important that people come to understand just how much our difficulties can vary according to all of the factors influencing us at any one time.

50: Faced up to going out in the first storm of the season for my daily walk; exhausting weather adds to the extra effort it takes autistic people to make all the decisions involved in going out especially when not for a specific reason such as an appointment. The wind dropped, rain stopped, sun came out and the Royal Scotsman train was in the station!

The validity of exhaustion added by bad weather can feel diluted by the fact we British people are known for being preoccupied by all things meteorological. It is very real. Wind and rain sting the skin and eyes; damp clothing chafes; brushing tangled hair hurts. All of these sensations are familiar to most people but it must be remembered that autistic people often have increased sensitivity. In Scotland we often talk about getting all four seasons in one day; this is not a big exaggeration. The temperature and other conditions truly can vary that much in that short a time. With a lower range of temperature tolerance and heightened sensory sensitivity, not only the effects themselves but all the decisions which must be made as to appropriate clothing for the day are indeed exhausting.

51: Spending time working on ideas to benefit other autistic people takes me back to when my own diagnosis was new and exciting; it renews my resolve to keep using my experiences to help those who are struggling and feeling alone to find their way to the support I have.

It is a good thing and very satisfying to regularly examine our own experiences for anything we could be doing to reach out. Bad experiences can become more positive if we can use them to help ourselves and others.

52: Writing an email to a friend about a series of stressful events one day through the week made me realise a few things; it was entirely understandable that I or any autistic person would have been stressed by the stacking up of events, I didn't do as badly as I thought and I didn't let them curtail my plans.

It takes us longer to process our responses because absolutely everything gets through; we have to filter out what other people don't necessarily even notice. We feel our responses very deeply and for a long time. When several things happen one after another, sometimes because we are still trying to deal with something from earlier, this added on effect is also multiplied.

53: After missing out on any view of the full Harvest Moon because of thick clouds, I woke to find myself looking right at it, the first thing I saw when I opened my eyes. It only lasted a few precious seconds before the clouds covered it again and stayed. I feel incredibly blessed by those few magical moments in time.

Many of us have difficulty sleeping; it is so hard to make our brains shut down and allow us to relax enough to drift off to sleep. Then of course we wake up tired. It is a gift to be sufficiently stimulated by the surroundings to get up early and enjoy a blessed start to the day.

54: Seeing a friend of mine and fellow planning group member talking on the news about autism gave me such a feeling of pride, both in my friend (who is also autistic) and in what we have achieved as a group and since then with our colleagues and contacts.

I have a horror of being recorded or filmed. It's fortunate that we don't all have the same aversions! In 2016 I eventually faced my fear to give a presentation which was not only filmed but webcast live. I talked about what it is like to participate in events as an autistic person; the effort it takes, the hard work we put in to getting it right, the personal investment in terms of our energy, anxiety, processing, overload and recovery time afterwards. In short, we try our best because we care so much and are so aware of the existence of pitfalls. Leaving at the end of the event, I spoke with a contact whose opinion meant a lot to me. Our worlds were too far apart to call it a friendship and we had not always agreed, but we had a rapport. They hugged me (with my consent), then told me, "Be careful". At that moment something died inside me. This was not the standard well-wishing "take care" or "mind how you go" type of greeting which people often use when saying goodbye. It was an actual warning; either a correction or an anticipation of my getting something wrong through not trying hard enough. It felt like an enormous betrayal of what they knew I had asked and given of myself that day for the sake of informing people just how much care we pour into everything we do. Sometimes we try too hard. It can feel at times as though

I spend half my life being branded incautious and the other half being accused of overthinking. My relationship with this person was never the same again. I stepped back from networking and eventually cut contact. I admit it was cowardly that I never told them exactly why, nor did I ask what they felt the need to caution me about on what should have been one of the most triumphant days of my life. The truth is I didn't want to know; I still don't. Imagining the embarrassment of hearing how I gave cause for this painfully timed vote of no confidence from someone I so admired makes me too queasy. I typically struggle with lack of clarity and closure so it is unusual for me not to seek it but some unexpected wounds to the spirit are just too sore when felt with autistic intensity. It may well be that I ought to have turned it into a learning opportunity; I have indeed learned from many of my experiences and will continue to do so but that one will have to be left alone.

55: Sent a Facebook message to catch up with my next door neighbour as her busy schedule, my bad timing and reluctance to try again for fear of looking needy have stopped us seeing one another for weeks or even months at a time. Felt ridiculous using that medium to contact someone so close that she could just about hear me typing, but it was worth it to make the gesture.

I still say it's ridiculous! However sometimes we have to compromise and adapt to a world which doesn't operate according to autistic logic in order to make important connections and relationships work for both parties. It is becoming more and more difficult for people to fit into one another's lives even without the social wariness attached to a lifetime of autistic misunderstandings. When a friendship is genuine and both parties are keen to maintain it, we find ways to make it work.

56: Unexpectedly met someone I knew from my last full time job (before moving long distance) who was on holiday in the Highlands. This was very unsettling as it reminded me of a very bad time and in fact this person when drunk picked an argument with me at my own 30th birthday work night out. However I was able to deal calmly with the encounter, she was perfectly pleasant and it reminded me how good a place I am in now, in every sense.

It was a plus that I recognised her so quickly. Recognising people out of context, even those close to us, can be a problem and it feels soul destroying when we have to deal with incredulity and offence over and over. Face blindness is becoming more understood as one of the ways in which autism can affect processing. It isn't always practical to warn every new person we meet that we might not recognise them immediately in the future! The increasing support for alert cards and other documents setting out the main points of our individual difficulties is a helpful trend.

57: Watching a well known classical singer in concert on TV telling stories of events in her career including one about an attack of cramp in front of the Queen Mother was a very encouraging reminder that "cringe moments" are not exclusive to autistic people; everyone can relate and they do not have to take away from anyone's attractiveness or success, autistic or not. It is equally important to remember that autism is so much more than the negative cliché of awkward moments.

Although the celebrity involved in this story is not autistic, there have been several examples of famous people revealing a diagnosis recently. Their courage as they take that enormous readjustment process into the public domain to help others is to be hugely respected.

The Inverness-bound Highland Chieftain
pulls into Aviemore Station as a ScotRail
Edinburgh service waits to leave

58: There was a fine, icy mist this morning not even enough to see but I could feel the minute ice crystals on my skin. It felt as though the air were sparkling. I know many people dread the winter and indeed there are aspects of it I dread, but I am so lucky to find all season changes exciting and feel anticipation from a grey sky.

Sensory sensitivity can be a bonus when it makes us experience nature more fully. I like the longer hours of darkness in winter; the streetlights are on, the moon and stars are more visible and there's always the hope that I will eventually see the Northern Lights in real life. The weather can be hard work to cope with but even in winter there are good calm spells. It can also be bad at any time of year!

59: Stood on the footbridge at Aviemore station this evening and watched the silver lines of light flowing along the track from the headlights of the approaching Highland Chieftain; had just been in Inverness to visit the HOSS six months to the day since it opened. So much has already been achieved and the team and everyone else involved's vision lights our way on.

The track to the south of Aviemore Station curves gently off to the right as you look from the footbridge. Before you see the train itself you see the rails light up from the approaching headlights. The light flows towards you; it looks magical and alive.

60: Having a much needed quiet day, letting it sink in how much I enjoy the peace of my neutrally decorated living room, soothing green of the bedroom and cheery blue of the kitchen. Outside, the streetlights are keeping their silent vigil and at this time and place all is calm.

These "grounded moments" are very important and central to the concept of mindfulness. We need to learn to focus on the present and allow a basic, uncluttered appreciation of what we have. These moments stay with us.

61: Heard beautiful guitar playing and singing coming from the HOSS music group today. It was a privilege to be around to hear such talent but even more so to sense the freedom of expression and spirit which allows people to come and feel enabled to play and sing.

There is an amazing wealth of talent among the people who use the HOSS. We have artists, dancers, musicians, singers and people who produce wonderful crafts and cooking. It is unthinkable that so much of this talent could have remained unrealised but it takes a proven safe environment to let people shine out into a society which can be so out of step with what we need in order to flourish.

62: Had a good chat with one of my friends at the station when I booked some train tickets. We were talking about the Disabled Person Railcards and how some conditions are not immediately obvious so people should never be questioned about having a Railcard. It was a good opportunity to increase understanding.

Having an "invisible" disability or condition carries the disadvantage of strangers not knowing to make allowances. It is exhausting to live with but we are fortunate to live in a time when, largely thanks to the Internet, awareness as the first step towards acceptance is increasing all the time. Awareness in itself is not enough but as the foundation of acceptance it can be a positive.

63: Remembering when I was diagnosed and told that the important thing to hold on to while getting used to it was that I am still the same person; it isn't a change that has just happened but a new perspective on how I have always been. It felt like coming home and starting again.

Diagnosis, especially later in life, can feel as though we have been put back to our factory settings. Everything is reset into a new context. It is scary; it is wonderful. With the right support, it is the start of our true life. That is the key thought to focus on as we adjust; we haven't changed. We are who we have always been.

64: All the standing lamps and fairy lights were lit at the HOSS today as it was such a dark grey afternoon. The autism friendly lighting gave such a soft, comforting glow, it was like being at home. Perfect for a gloomy day.

As a child I always found soft, warm lighting on a dark grey late afternoon especially cosy and loved reading descriptions of it in stories. I think I associated it with the relief of getting away from the harshness of the school day, which I now recognise as overload. I read Charles Dickens and wished I could have been a lamplighter. I wouldn't have been so keen to get up early and switch them all off again though!

65: Arrived home from an overnight trip away to go out with local and visiting friends; I had a good chat about a complicated situation which has been worrying me due to my autistic inability to read people. I have been made to see that I've done better than I thought and bonded even more closely with my friends.

We should beware of falling into the trap of automatically expecting to fail at something because we are autistic; it is worth at least questioning to ourselves, with support when needed, whether it really is inevitable. At the same time, any disability does come with certain limitations; some fluctuating, some constant. Those limitations often come not from the disability but from an inaccessible setting. Nevertheless, it is nobody's place to tell any ill or disabled person not to let their condition define them, hold them back or any similar dismissive phrase when the person is honest about something being a problem. Neither is shaming them by quoting examples of someone else who did so much better despite the same or worse barriers. This is ableism and diminishes a daily struggle which is not for anyone else to judge. That includes others with the same condition and those who believe they fully understand how the condition affects everyone who has it because they know someone with it. We are all different and have our own limits. Listening, asking what has already been tried and if appropriate offering suggestions in an encouraging and respectful way then listening some more is the way to help us to explore our potential.

66: Treated to an enchanted light show in my garden first thing in the morning as a robin landed in the lilac tree and dislodged a whole load of dew, which caught the low sun as it showered to the ground. It looked magical.

One of the more enjoyable aspects of autism for many of us is keeping a level of imagination generally associated with childhood. It is a creative gift which should not be confused with immaturity. When I had to move house unexpectedly and found accommodation available in Nairn, I had never even been to the town, only through it on the train. So, and I mean absolutely no disrespect by this to beautiful Nairn and its friendly people, I was struggling. As an autistic person moving from a place I loved and already knew well before living there to somewhere completely unknown to me, it was a huge life upheaval to have to cope with. I created a theme for this new chapter in my life; I was merely popping through the back of the wardrobe to Nairnia. Like most of my generation I read the classic novels by C S Lewis, The Chronicles of Narnia, as a child. They even dovetailed neatly with my love of streetlights as the first landmark encountered by the Pevensie children on discovering Narnia is a lamp post which becomes an ongoing part of the mythology. It just so happens that there are a lot of similarly designed ones in Nairn; on the path leading from the station and one wonderfully visible from my flat. My landlord Allan became Aslan. It all makes me smile even as I go about all the very prosaic realities of being an adult and a householder.

67: Watching one of the best science fiction films, it is good to be reminded just how vast the universe is and that in all of infinite space the most important thing we can do is find our own answers and help others.

I was always fascinated by space and still love the night sky, for its aesthetic beauty and for the sense of comforting perspective it gives. I have enjoyed many a philosophical, setting the world to rights conversation with my good friend Ann on her visits from Edinburgh as we sit outside looking at the stars. We were doing just that when I realised thanks to her smartphone apps that I was knowingly looking at Saturn for the first time in my life. I wonder whether any race on another planet has its equivalent of autism. I hope so as it adds such colour and insight to the collective intelligence and creativity of any species and it gets things done. Our eventually contacting and learning from another world may depend on it.

68: I was complimented on my manners as I stood up to shake hands when introduced to someone. It made me feel I am not so isolated after all in a world where manners are becoming so rare, they are beginning to be mistaken for social reticence or weakness! (Important note: nobody, including children, should be coerced into physical contact they do not want, unless it is to remove them from danger.)

Of course I can sometimes go the other way and be blunt without meaning to; judging tone and volume can be a problem. That doesn't mean I lack the principles of politeness. It saddens me that we live in a world where opening a door slowly to avoid battering anyone who may be coming from the other side is seen as timidity rather than common sense. There are still times when hope is restored. On a train in England several years ago a hen party joined the carriage I was in at Newcastle; my heart sank at the potential noise, though I willingly made room for one of them to sit next to me. Naturally she was turning around to talk to her friends; I was a complete stranger, yet she apologised to me for turning her back. Moments like that inspire me to keep on fighting the impulse to withdraw when the bad times get too much and to keep paying attention to these fleeting interactions with others as I have experienced what a difference a bit of effort or a gesture of goodwill can make to someone's day.

69: After an unusually long (and frustrating) wait, the winter season lights finally returned to Aviemore. I feel part of my spirit is stored in them; my energy improves when they return. I love the contradiction of the fleeting, icy transience of snowflakes captured in a warm, steady familiar light.

Autistic people can love things or places with an intensity that feels like a living friendship. I feel that I am sharing a conspiratorial awareness with Aviemore as the trademark ski season lights return; while so many people are seeing only the end of the summer they love, we are coming fully to life as Aviemore comes into its own. (2018 footnote: Even though I have moved since this was written, my regular visits to Aviemore mean that I still get to track the seasonal progression of light across that mountain skyline. The travelling can be a challenge but I have the support of Flora, Jeni and all of my Aviemore family and friends. It is a blessing to have built such a strong network by the time I had to move on.)

70: A friend I am going to visit and stay with for a couple of nights in early December in Edinburgh is taking precious annual leave for my visit, putting her Christmas decorations up early. I must have demonstrated social skills at some point to get and keep such a friend.

Reciprocal friendships with give and take on both sides are to be treasured and never taken for granted. Bridget is one of the best; a true diamond who will be there to the end and there is no limit to her giving.

71: Went out for the first time in a few days after a bout of ill health. Fresh air, seeing people I know and making train and restaurant bookings for plans over the next few weeks gave me a feeling of coming back to life.

Sensory and fatigue issues mean that autistic people can experience enhanced effects from everyday illnesses such as colds and headaches. This is another way in which we are not always given the space, understanding and adjustments we need, by ourselves as much as by others.

72: After an exhausting, wasted day I arrived home with a broken umbrella in heavy rain feeling totally wiped out. Then I braced myself to tackle replacing a household fixture and managed it; as I went out to put the packaging in the recycling bin, the storm had passed leaving a starry sky.

This kind of activity, however satisfying, can set us back if we attempt too much too soon during recovery time after having been ill. It is important to do a bit at a time and keep a close guard on energy levels, hydration and nutrition.

73: Had an unexpectedly inclusive text message today! Pleasantly surprised to find that when I am not able to be around to do things my way, others are prepared to continue my creative quirks and take the time and trouble to ask me. Uplifting HOSS solidarity!

I should have known better than to be surprised. This is entirely in keeping with the HOSS' principles and ethos.

74: Unpredictable factors can come up even going two minutes up the road to a GP appointment first thing in the morning; beautiful sunny frost so I had coffee in the garden, watched the Highland Chieftain go by then thought I would be late as first I had to stop a random cat getting into the house when I put my cup back inside, then the gate was frozen shut. I wasn't late and I had a laugh with the doctor about it; a routine chore turned colourful.

Seeing the funny side and enjoying randomness can be a massively helpful coping mechanism in stressful times. Mornings like that, much as it made me laugh, also remind us to do ourselves a favour by always allowing plenty of time to do what we need to. We cannot predict everything that might delay us even on a short errand, such as having to make sure we don't lock someone else's cat in the house!

75: Having very vivid dreams while routine disrupted by being away from home. It is always a relief to wake up and establish familiarity with surroundings once again. At the same time it is quite exciting seeing what my subconscious will come up with next!

I wonder whether autism makes people dream more intensely. It seems logical we would have our own range of traits to our dreams, though non-autistic family and friends have told me plenty of colourful and bizarre dreams they had!

76: Helped out with some gift wrapping as part of one of my voluntary jobs; I was dreading it as I worried I would not be fast enough and would hold the others up but it actually went well and we finished ahead of schedule.

Manual dexterity is a major pitfall; I find I can never be quick enough and when it is added to trying to keep up socially in a group situation where I don't want to disclose my autism because I don't know the people and won't see them often, it increases the pressure. I was lucky with that group; we all cooperated to find a way of working which suited everyone and got the job done with no disclosure necessary. I often have to remind myself not to assume people will react negatively or create barriers.

77: Having a random thought while waiting for a scan to finish on my computer and let me get on with my day. If Marie Antoinette really did say "Let them eat cake" when told the people had no bread, she was either being flippant or it could have the interpretation of an early example of autistic literal understanding!

I doubt whether she really did say it and if she did, I'm sure she was being sarcastic. Many autistic people do have difficulty with sarcasm but I am a bit too good at it!

78: Had a frustrating shopping trip wherein two simple transactions turned long and complicated with people kept waiting behind me because of other people's mistakes. It was stressful because of the building queues but I managed to make appropriate small talk both times, fighting the urge to withdraw and freeze.

It is important to clarify that I wanted to be able to chat in that situation. Had I not wanted to and allowed myself to feel guilty or less valid because of it, that would be an example of sacrificing autism acceptance to please a society which is geared towards social performance. Having very high standards and wanting everything to be done right is an asset in some ways but a drawback in others. We cannot control what other people do and we can end up under a lot of unnecessary stress feeling responsible for the smooth running of everything around us. When people I know are visiting the area, I feel guilty if the weather turns bad! It's so important to keep a sense of perspective.

79: A beautiful "signalman's morning", as my favourite railway author Adrian Vaughan describes bright still frosty autumn mornings. Took coffee outside to watch the Chieftain go by and discovered the return of sparkly bin season. One of my most popular Facebook posts last year was about the frost making the bins sparkle and how wonderful to be inspired by something as mundane as putting the rubbish out. Love autistic detail!

Those who know me are well used to my enthusing about things like signalman's mornings and sparkly bin season. It seems all positive to me that it gives such a lift to what I appreciate for many people must be a depressing chore; putting the bins out on darkening evenings and particularly the first time the lids are frozen shut. My status had also mentioned that and prising the lid open with a shovel; I got an excellent tip from Mandi next door. One good thump right in the centre of the lid pops it open.

80: Did some research after talking to people at the HOSS and feel much more settled in my mind about dealing with a potential secondary diagnosis added to my autism, which had disturbed me. Their perspective is vital.

Other conditions such as personality disorders can coexist with autism but it is always an upheaval to have a new label to cope with. It is vital to have a good, informed support system which will help us to get clarification, to question and challenge when we need to and to make sure other professionals understand our autism. We need to be able to make the most of our appointments and understanding ourselves is fundamental to this. Knowledge of autism is generally improving; a welcome trend but we have to work on it and keep up that momentum.

81: Had a really good long online chat with a good friend who said she had noticed a few changes in me lately; she had started some online games with other friends and worried I would see the updates and assume I'd been left out, which once I would have, but thanks to autism support I had rationalised and knew otherwise.

I have so often been guilty of expecting the worst and making preemptive strikes, pushing people away before they can do it to me. It is something with which I still struggle and always will. In this case, I realised that the reason my friend was playing this game with other people and not me was that in order to be in the game, which involves people posting cartoons in which they can feature their friends, you had to have created a profile for yourself on the app for it, which I hadn't so there was no cartoon of me for her to use. Before I had the support I do now, I may well not have gotten as far as figuring that out; I would only have seen the exclusion I am primed to expect. After our chat, Karen posted a cartoon about rushing for the train to visit her Scottish pal; I keep it as a reminder of the benefit of stopping myself thinking the worst.

82: Walking at dusk on an ideal late autumn evening, there was a layer of fine white mist over the fields in the distance. At first it was hard to tell whether it was fog or smoke from the moorland controlled burning. It got me thinking, autism so often draws a veil over how we can perceive the emotions and situations behind a person's expression or apparent demeanour; hot or cold, but often all we need to do is walk peacefully alongside.

Trying to read and understand others' feelings and react in the right way is an uphill struggle at times. We struggle because we have empathy! What we are more likely to get wrong is picking up on others' intentions, motives and expectations. Because of the ways in which we have been told we are limited, we ask more of ourselves than we should. We task ourselves with somehow knowing details which are not available to us and may indeed be none of our business, yet we infer from not knowing those details that we are wrong. Sometimes the best thing we can do is let it be; get on with what we need to do, be pleasant and polite and let others reach out to us in their own time.

83: Taking photos in Falcon Square in Inverness on a deep blue twilight, someone else was also taking photos and as we changed places to get the variety of views, we exchanged nods and smiles; a shared understanding, co-operation and camaraderie. Lovely moment.

Some moments like this are to be enjoyed just for what they are with no follow-up. When I was much younger I was too eager to latch on to every friendly interaction as a potential friendship; I tried too hard and sometimes scared people off. When I was in the sixth form and applying to universities, I went to an open day and got talking to three other girls, none of whom knew each other. I cannot remember the conversation but they were relaxed, taking the day as it came while I was too keen to impress and desperate to bond after a largely isolated childhood. As we all went to the lecture theatre, the stewards were asking people at the door how many seats together they required; the girls I had latched onto immediately all said "Three" just as I said "Four". I let them go; I resignedly asked for one seat. It took a few years for me to figure out where I had gone wrong and to acknowledge that their way of dealing with it was rude and cruel but they were just starting out as adults and learning too. It is largely due to the support I have received since my diagnosis that I got better at balancing interaction and self reliance. I can see one-off moments for what they are.

84: Really good meeting at the HOSS today; felt a sense of regained perspective and it was a revelation to be told I am doing well by being able to recognise and speak up for my support needs, as opposed to being considered as wrong by more mainstream services.

Non autism specific services, however well intentioned, are often difficult and inaccessible places for us to turn. Not because they are bad; they are just not designed in the best way for us and people don't know how to approach us. A lot of valuable work is being done to bridge this gap in understanding by improving the training and information available about autism, making it up to date and locally relevant. Those of us who can speak up should also try to advocate by amplifying the voices of those who cannot, as well as for ourselves. I am fortunate enough to know and be friends with some remarkable people involved in this work.

85: Packing for a few days away; I always try to minimise luggage due to worrying about not being quick and dexterous enough and getting in people's way, annoying them. This time I am having to face those fears and carry a bit extra so that after a year of health problems, disappointments and bad news, my mother will have some luxuries in our holiday apartment. Feeling proud.

Isn't it interesting, and telling, that I could make myself push my limits only because it was to benefit someone else. The instinct to justify begins in many an autistic childhood and it takes a lot of support and hard work beyond diagnosis to unravel it.

Falcon Square, Inverness

86: Counted out some change to the value of my usual drink at a local place and had it ready in a plastic money bag before leaving the house as the loose, heavy silver in my purse was getting out of control, because I hand over notes so as not to delay people by struggling to get hold of coins. It was a practical solution, gave me a conversation starter and the change was appreciated.

This has been a big problem all my life and I have read of other autistic people having similar experiences; for some reason coins are very difficult to get and keep hold of. We should give ourselves due credit for the coping strategies we have had to develop and use discreetly in what are entirely unremarkable, basic scenarios to many people. When a magician performs a trick, he isn't really doing magic; he isn't really breaking the laws of physics. What he is doing is getting around them by distracting the audience without them realising it, so that they look the other way and then see what they came to see. Their perspective is redirected just enough, then the rabbit is pulled out of the hat; the chosen card drawn from the pack with a flourish; the coin plucked from behind the ear of the astonished volunteer. That subtle but crucial distraction is the real magic; it is a finely tuned skill and it is hard work. So many autistic people have had to develop a similar level of performing, often without even realising, just to get through the day. We must give ourselves more credit.

87: Spent some time today in the HOSS looking at some of the autism library books. There were accounts in them which described some of the difficulties and the misunderstandings involved in living with autism and it was so reassuring that it's not just me. Such a vital environment for sharing.

I wholeheartedly salute each and every autistic person who has found the courage to share their cringe moments not only with other people but in the public domain, in the spirit of helping others to recognise that they are not alone. It helps to understand that sometimes we have been overthinking every word and every possible direction the conversation could take afterwards for so long, that part of us takes a break and we just go for it. Throw in a bit of sheer bad luck and you have the moments which stay with us long after the others involved have forgiven and forgotten; often for the rest of our lives. I will never forget the day I pointed out a couple of mildly amusing surnames on a database in the privacy of a small office only to find that one of the people was a friend of the colleague sitting next to me. To my shame I couldn't even manage to apologise; my colleague was matter of fact and seemed only mildly offended but I simply couldn't speak and struggled to face anyone all day.

88: Out shopping today it was the kind of day where I feel fragile and exposed for no one definable reason and it makes me extra wary of people. I compensated by being extra smiley and forcing myself to focus on being a positive aspect of the day everyone I interacted with was having, on the basis that it wouldn't help me or anyone else if my feelings impacted on them. I got home feeling more relaxed, despite having to cope with handfuls of change!

Shopping and coping with public places in general is becoming more difficult as the pace of life increases; the important thing to remember is that in general, people don't bear us any malice and are just focused on getting through the day as we are. Just like us, they sometimes misjudge. Waiting to be served in a narrow aisle in a local shop, I just knew that the woman in front of me was going to turn around rapidly and carelessly to dash for the door;

there was no room for me to take evasive action. By the time I had checked there was nobody close enough behind me to prevent a quick step backwards, she had already spun around, her hurried energy swooping into my personal space. She did a spectacular double-take at my unexpected presence, jarring my ears with a loud, almost operatic "OH!!! Sorreeeeeeeeeeee!" She truly didn't mean any harm and couldn't have known how harsh it was to my already heightened senses. It felt as though my brain had been put in a cocktail shaker full of white noise, given a really good shoogle as we say in Scotland and the swirling mixture poured back into a head which felt as brittle as glass. She had been talking to the cashier about having cold tootsies from wearing sandals on what turned out a much colder day than it looked. It happened that I was in the same situation; somehow I managed to turn that into a friendly remark to diffuse the turmoil inside. I was lucky that time. Such an outwardly trivial happening can affect us so strongly. I should emphasise that this is a memory which came to me as I added this particular positive thought to my book; the occurrence in the shop had happened in the summer. People do not tend to wear sandals when out shopping in December in Scotland!

89: At the darkest time of year, a week before the solstice, I was just thinking that the solar powered fairy lights in my garden probably wouldn't come on at all today and thinking how special it will be to watch them respond as the light grows towards Spring. Then I glanced outside and they were shining brightly in the 3pm dusk.

The interludes when my solar lights come on in the winter are precious for their brevity. They get so little chance to charge up and then the dark hours outlast that small reserve of light by such a margin it is hard to imagine them shining all night with energy to spare. There are times in life like that and we need to be able to supplement our resources in other ways. This includes support and also reminding ourselves of when things have gone well; writing about it, reminiscing about it with people we trust and listening when others remind us of our value.

90: Having to deal with some potential disruption and short notice changes to a planned journey, I am drawing upon a lot of techniques I have learned to refine through involvement with the HOSS; keeping calm, getting all the facts, not being too impulsive and remembering to share information with others travelling.

I almost spent a lot of extra money booking an overnight stay and making the most at risk part of the journey early. As well as the uncertainty, I was influenced by the memory of when a similar journey was drastically delayed, leading to me having to make calls on my mobile phone to relay information to the people expecting me despite no chance of hearing the person on the other end because of the noise around me. In the end, this journey was nowhere near as bad as I had feared.

91: Arrived at the family home for Christmas; a mixed blessing as we get on but they do not know about my diagnosis. Seeing the fairy lights evoked pleasure in the routine of switching on the upstairs ones every afternoon; marking the passing days and enjoying cosy evenings.

It is difficult having to hide my diagnosis from elderly parents who are in poor health and would struggle with the upheaval of their only child's life being given an entirely new perspective. It may give them some answers but I have had to make the call that the upset of going over the past and coming to terms with not having known something so fundamental about me right from the start, as well as the realisation that something had gone drastically wrong in my life leading me to be referred and assessed, would be too much given their age and health. Many people judge me for that decision but those people have usually never even met my parents; I have to be true to my own knowledge and experience. So I watch what I say, cope with every outing in the hope there won't be too many awkward moments and keep my eyes on the positives.

92: Had to face packed supermarket with family on last Saturday before Christmas. We ended up having such a laugh as it took two assistants to get the security tag off a bottle of malt whisky, pulling it like a cracker and everyone cheered when it came off. It had been very grey and damp when we set out but we emerged into blue skies and a winter solstice rainbow.

Marking each solstice and equinox is a big part of my year; I love the contrast of each extreme of light and dark in the Summer and Winter and the graceful natural handover of the seasons as everything aligns in the Spring and Autumn. In the Scottish Highlands, the fluctuation between light and dark hours means that it can be light until 11pm in the summer and dark soon after 3pm in the winter. At each solstice the opposite season seems so mysterious and far away; as my solar fairy lights come on at 3pm I can hardly believe that there really will be a time I'm still waiting for them to come on after 11pm. It gives me the variety within familiarity that I crave.

93: Reminiscing today about a train journey where I saw a young woman across the aisle endure the kind of scenario I dread and get stressed about when booking seats; she was booked at a table with three strangers who were settled in, had to ask them to move to let her and luggage in and one of them spilt their drink in doing so which made the poor lass feel awkward. Empathising led me to share some whisky miniatures which were a birthday gift and it led to a memorable, convivial journey.

That had been a difficult week away; I had, among other issues, faced eating related taunts from strangers in a pub which echoed things I last heard said to me at primary school. My coping skills were down to survival only. However, in these circumstances empathy and the overwhelming wish that nobody else had to feel the way I do can unlock a hidden level of my consciousness and allow me to step up. Especially when I'm on the Chieftain, my magical train! An American couple on their first trip to the Highlands was introduced to an 18 year old single malt at the precise moment we crossed Druimuachdar Pass summit and they officially entered the Highlands. Moderation is important when drinking alcohol but such pleasures and responsibilities can be part of a healthy life.

The northbound Highland Chieftain approaching Aviemore

94: Interesting conversation comparing experiences of people, especially children, with undiagnosed conditions such as autism or dyslexia to films where there is a ghost or a monster causing mischief and disbelieving adults punish the children. How difficult for those who have been living their whole lives like that, suffering at school and home then socially as they grow, and what a blessing the increase in services and autism acceptance is.

Some people firmly believe in ghosts; others categorically don't. I have an open mind. I have often wondered, though, whether there could be a theory that the autistic brain's focus, capacity for intense attachment to places and liking for repetitive activity could make us more susceptible to haunting our old routines... It could be a wonderful conversation to have late at night with good friends in a softly lit snug!

95: It is Christmas Day. Colours, sensory input of all kinds are completely different from usual. It is indeed rich and strange; I am enjoying the novelty and looking forward to getting back to routine. I know this is a blessing as many people will feel flat when it is over. Thinking of those for whom it is a difficult time; for every down in life there is a corresponding up.

I enjoy the run-up to Christmas more than the day itself. The colours and lights and scents can be too much for autistic people; I am fortunate enough to enjoy them and find them exciting. The social expectations, crowds and disrupted routine are less appealing and the vast majority of Christmas songs are not to my taste! However I love the sparkle and warmth, the crackle of a log fire, the scent of cloves and pine and cinnamon. Aviemore glitters with a fine latticework of lights all year round; the ski season lights stay up until Easter and many buildings have fairy lights around their Scandinavian style roofs which are just as in keeping with late summer twilight.

96: Looking through a book I gave elderly relatives for Christmas, I learned the meaning of some social networking abbreviations; I knew some already but it was a bonus learning the others in such an unobtrusive way and this is a very feelgood method of doing it. Including others rather than assume it wouldn't be their thing is a prime example of treating people how I would like to be treated myself; an ethic I try to live by.

It is a myth that autistic people are always formal and never join in with trends or popular culture. I admit I struggle to find a middle ground with my writing style; when criticised for a document I produced being far too wordy, I confided in a trusted colleague that I only do three styles; formal, colloquial and profane. Only one of those was suitable for the piece of work in question. I am working on it; as an autistic person myself, I find myself guilty of unforgivably betraying my own community if I fail to make such pieces of work accessible to all.

97: Had to use a bit of social subterfuge to gently encourage some visitors to leave as my mother was clearly becoming tired but is too polite to make her excuses and rest. I said she had better watch the time for her lunch so she could take her painkillers; the guests took the hint and picked up the social cue. Contrary to stereotyping, such skills aren't closed to autistic people.

I will never deny or play down the difficulties I and many other autistic people have with picking up social cues, reading between the lines and so on. It is important, though, to balance that out and remember that not only do we all vary in our profile of symptoms but those symptoms themselves can vary from occasion to occasion. Many a time I have had to stay quiet because all things considered, the risk of saying the wrong thing was just too great. I have no doubt sometimes this was the right decision and sometimes I should have been braver. Sometimes saying the wrong thing is not the worst that could happen.

98: Doing my Hogmanay rituals of writing all the birthdays, anniversaries etc on next year's calendar and filing away this year's personal letters and cards, recycling all the older correspondence, is a lovely autism friendly way to finish off and tidy up the year as well as reminding myself to appreciate the people in my life and the organisation of my own space and anticipate next year.

Hogmanay (the Scottish name for New Year's Eve) is a distinctive watershed for me as an autistic person; I don't join crowded street parties but I enjoy the atmosphere of celebration. It being a double bank holiday in Scotland on the first two days of January, it marks one last chance to appreciate being at home relaxing and recharging after Christmas before the return to normal routine which is always very welcome by that point.

One of the "Nairnia" lamp posts

99: I had posted a status on Facebook about not being any good at coming up with clever and original words of comfort during a year of constant bad news; that I had been focusing on my work and hoping to do my bit by bringing better news of areas in which I can make a difference, as I am a more practical person. The response has been amazing from friends telling me I have in fact been there for them and helped. Being very fixed in my self image it took all the willpower I possess not to protest at some calling me young; I'm over 40!, but I held back.

It can be so difficult to keep a sense of perspective when our intense responses are out of step with the intention behind what is being said to us. It would have been very ungracious of me to protest at people calling me young when it was incidental to encouraging comments and I realise that many people, especially women, prefer to be thought of as young. Like many autistic people I have always been drawn towards older people and felt I had little in common with my own age group especially before my diagnosis; at the same time I look younger than I am, so I end up feeling hypersensitive about being taken seriously as an adult. When a 70 year old friend calls me young, I can just about deal with it; when it comes from people within a few years either way of my age, it can be a tad annoying! I am glad to say on that occasion I managed to let better instincts prevail; I admit I don't always. That said, many of us have things like this which cause deep hurt when they are said to us again and again; if someone tells you that something you said hurt them, that must be respected. It is despicable to laugh in their face and say it again! That seems obvious, yet it has been done to me and my fellow autistic people many times. Neither should the person be ordered to take it as a compliment. They may have had years of being talked over and devalued for looking young. Likewise, defining them by the accent they have worked hard for decades to change, however much you like that accent, may have propelled them straight back into an incredibly painful past. If they say it hurt them, it hurt them; make amends.

100: Heard about the possibility of a new group being formed at the HOSS, following on from the existing and very successful late diagnosis group. People attending this group have connected with others who have similar experiences, in a way they would not have otherwise. Such an exciting development.

I simply cannot overstate the importance and joy of those moments we realise "It's not just me after all!", especially sharing in a guaranteed safe environment.

101: Another stressful benefits milestone today but as I was coming into the HOSS, I still managed to help a lady get to her connecting train at Inverness when there were only a few minutes before it departed. The team at the HOSS was very supportive and made me feel good about that achievement.

That acknowledgement and praise for the times we achieve something when our circumstances makes it extra difficult is so important. It encourages us to keep fighting on and it reminds us how big these achievements are.

102: I have always been wary of group situations but have decided to attend the late diagnosis group at the HOSS. It is a big step but the team and my associated friends have given me the courage and confidence boost to take the chance next time it is on at a time I am free.

Groups in general are difficult as they so often tend to break down into multiple conversations which makes it hard to hear what is being said. There are also the anxieties around saying the wrong thing, speaking just as someone else also begins to speak, showing our processing delays by asking a question which was answered while we were thinking about what to say and so on. Nervousness can cause us to giggle inappropriately and this can lead to misunderstandings. Sensitive, non-blame orientated and compassionate moderation is very important, as is the availability of a nearby but separate quiet room or outdoor space as a retreat if a participant becomes distressed.

103: A special day; the anniversary of my diagnosis of autism being confirmed. It was such a positive thing for me as it gave me answers, access to support and solidarity with other autistic people and a whole new perspective. I celebrate it as my "other birthday", though not being the Queen I don't expect to have my second birthday marked by anything more than texts from my close friends!

It is always interesting to hear about other autistic people's perspectives on this; whether or not they celebrate their diagnosis anniversary, how they mark it and what they call it. I have heard that I am not the only one to mark the occasion. I am quite lucky too in that mine falls in mid January, the opposite time of year to my birthday and just into that flat, dark spell after Christmas when so many people are not enjoying the time of year it affects the whole atmosphere.

104: I feel I have made some progress this week in coming to better understand that not everyone has my autistic attention to detail and memory which makes me so particular about keeping promises and not forgetting arrangements or contact at significant times. Expecting others to do the same for me and feeling let down when they don't is sometimes like being disappointed when a dog doesn't miaow.

Our attention to detail and precise memory can be a drawback when we are already prone to feeling isolated and cannot naturally relate to the fact others don't necessarily have the same intensity of focus. We have friends who care very much in their own way; it's just that remembering significant times and dates isn't what they do. We feel forgotten and take it personally; we can end up feeling that it would be better if we didn't tell anyone about our significant anniversaries and so on then we won't be disappointed. We feel we are always the ones making the effort. Sometimes we are. It is a weight off our minds if we can come to terms with the fact some people just process life differently and learn to recognise the other ways they show they care.

105: Opened the back door to a quiet night with no wind, just cool air and white streetlights shining on bare tree branches full of mist and the remnants of a shower. It looked and felt completely peaceful. This has been another uneventful day with feelings of emptiness, but that simple pleasure was enough.

We tend to appreciate and bind ourselves firmly to our routines. However, when that is combined with our intensity of feeling and emotion, a feeling of emptiness despite our wanting our routines the way they are is one of our many apparent contradictions. What often helps to provide bright moments on our empty days is the detail our senses take in and appreciate; we feel everything.

106: Sometimes following popular trends can have its advantages. After yet another stressful appointment, spent a good half hour in fits of laughter at a game on a social networking site where people are adding the words "Up Your Bum" to film titles. Going through my DVD collection, by the time I got to "The 39 Steps Up Your Bum" I was crying with laughter for the first time in many months.

Autistic people do have a sense of humour; we need it! We do get jokes. Literal interpretation can be an issue and get in the way but it isn't the all pervading feature of autism that many people think it is. Sometimes we get caught out; of course we do, but that it just as likely to be because of sensory overload, overthinking and processing everything around us so that we miss a vital cue. We get the joke; it can just take a few seconds longer for it to fall into place, making its way through our heightened processing of the sounds, smells and sights around us as if the snow in a snow globe were falling through glue instead of water. If we don't quite catch it, never write us off as someone to whom you cannot tell a joke or use a metaphor.

107: Just had fun out in the garden in the dark breaking up some polystyrene packaging for the rubbish, to help out my next door neighbour. I cannot stand touching the stuff and the cracking noise of the tiles breaking up was not very autism friendly!, but it livened up a rather flat day and helped a friend.

I love moments in time like that. Doing something a bit offbeat where I could potentially be seen by passers by felt exciting and even better for it being to help my pal. It seemed all the more quirky for it being pitch dark, though I hasten to add it wasn't the middle of the night; those tiles made quite a racket even without autistic sensitivity!

108: It started to snow when I was out for a walk and I loved the sudden stillness, the softness of the falling flakes and the sense of being alone with nature as it was quietly activated around me. Later on the sky was brilliantly intense at twilight; glowing turquoise with ice crystals in the high atmosphere.

I saw a month of these luminous opal skies at twilight when I stayed in Aviemore for most of November 2011. It was the luckiest I have been with weather in my entire life and got me writing poetry again. "With points of shadowed evergreen, you tap the frosted well of deepened dusk and autograph the skyline: AVIEMORE." I moved there from Edinburgh four months later. I knew I'd see a lot of different weather of course!

One of my favourite Aviemore photographs,
taken at Muirton: Manmade and natural.

109: Downloaded some music from groups I used to listen to many years ago, a different time in my life. Music is one of the most powerful stimuli for evoking memories and I enjoyed bringing back the good times, remembering selectively and bringing the best of those days into my current life, the new context giving the memory of the songs fresh associations.

The most powerful sense for evoking memories, however, is smell. It is fascinating how the brain, autistic or not, works and connects everything together. Looking at the physiological facts of ourselves can provide enlightenment and practical perspective when we feel overwhelmed by our emotional reactions to things going wrong.

110: Had to put up new curtain rails and had never done such a task before; I am not a DIY person but I am on my own so have no choice but to get on with it. Took me all afternoon at the expense of other tasks, left me exhausted and aching but I accomplished it.

We can acquire the necessary skills for things like the practical day to day running of a home. Achieving something safely and as independently as we can will always be rewarding, even if we don't enjoy it.

111: Nothing brightens up the flat void of yet another dark grey morning, after the streetlights have gone off, quite like the delivery of a new computer keyboard backlit in seven different colours to choose from!

I tried to resist because it felt a bit cliched but I did end up with a colour for each day of the week!

Taken from the footbridge at Nairn Station after a journey described in the March 2014 chapter

112: Went to a volunteers' lunch and sat with three lads I didn't know; they all knew each other. That, plus eating in front of strangers in a noisy room, plus a badly timed blizzard out of nowhere which meant everyone noticed my drookit* hair instead of my well chosen dressy outfit, could have added up to an autistic nightmare but I got into the conversation and overall it went well.
*Drookit is a Scots word which means "drenched".

Eating in front of other people is a complex issue for me. I am fine if it's people I know well and am relaxed around, but it can also be acceptable in a group of strangers; that depends on the circumstances. I cannot eat in front of anyone by whom I am overawed, even in an otherwise relaxed group. We are vulnerable when we are eating; we are not really on our dignity. I don't mind eating out alone but I dread the moment well meaning waiting staff lean over me and ask if everything is OK with my meal, inevitably when I have just taken a mouthful. I feel under pressure when anyone asks me questions when I'm eating. Pragmatic acceptance and low key, sincere adjustment to accommodate these traits is a vital feature of autism friendliness.

113: Produced a document at work which included designs and effects I had never seen how to publish before. I found it so satisfying figuring it out and managed to replicate every feature from the draft I was asked to copy. Loved becoming absorbed in working out how to do it and turning my attention to detail to getting it right.

This is one of the main areas in which autistic people can be an asset to employers. Attention to detail and a driven determination to get it just right are valuable work skills.

Not all of us can manage full time work but what we can do is wholehearted and thorough.

114: Walking home today I had a rare moment when for no apparent reason it suddenly hit me just how much I love living here. I am always aware of it, but every so often it overwhelms me with full-on autistic intensity without any particular trigger to which I can ascribe the feeling. It raised my energy for the day.

An unexpected celebratory moment can happen at any time and be a lovely surprise.

115: Had to repeat a journey to an appointment that went badly last time; it was cancelled, the message didn't reach me because I do not give out my mobile number for calls and I incurred needless expense on a day I was already tired and low. This time, I had a successful appointment and a good laugh with the taxi drivers both ways, almost missing Falcon Square on the way back as we were laughing so much about some joker having listed the Cairngorm Mountain funicular railway for sale on eBay!

This is sometimes referred to as "Getting back on the horse"; facing something again after it went wrong can be very daunting but also doubly rewarding.

116: Added dog treat flower arranging to my impulsive creative experiments, pushing some curled shaped ones onto stick shaped ones to make a "bouquet" for my neighbour's dogs after one of their fostered companions died. I am a cat person with a kitchen ponging of dog treats and with my usual bad timing I had to leave them on her doorstep, but I did have the presence of mind to anticipate this and take a photo. She loved it.

Creativity in unusual forms is often a feature of autism. Adapting our interactions with an unpredictable world to increase our chances of success is a skill we often refine without even realising it. The photo certainly came in useful as when my then neighbour came home, her dogs saw the gift first so the arrangement didn't last long!

117: Someone at work was asking for ideas on where he could get some specific printing done; I suggested somewhere nearby and he managed to get it done there. As I so often feel out of step with the world, it was a big moment to have one of my suggestions go right. Just as what seems small to some people can really distress me, fortunately it works out magnifying good times too.

We are all free to choose to appreciate anything, however small, which helps or makes us feel good.

118: Sat through a very difficult meeting which was preceded by a delayed journey and the shock of finding out an ally appeared to have turned against me; had to cope with the rapid flow of information and with being upstaged yet again, but I was told someone else present said I helped them greatly with my one timely intervention.

Autism is one very important thing we all have in common but we have to accept that we will not always get on or agree. Sometimes a rift is just too deep and painful to be resolved and we have to let it be even if we still have to see and interact with the person concerned, which can hurt very much. I am glad to say that in this case it was resolved and put behind us. Agreeing to disagree can be one of the most difficult things we have to do and require sensitive support which will take into account how much longer our deep feelings last than people may expect. It also requires not placing an ill-informed and unrealistic expectation on autistic people or any marginalised group that all members of that group will automatically be compatible, have the same goals or understand one another.

119: The day after a bad crisis, I coped better than I ever expected by calling the HOSS, checking on a friend who had also had a difficult day, doing some artwork personalising my ScotRail "KeepCup" (an environment friendly scheme where they sold reusable hot drink cups and gave a discount for their use on subsequent journeys), then went for a walk. I was asked for directions, which is a fear of mine but I managed and also remembered extra local information the people needed.

Everything else in this example became possible after that call to the HOSS. Informed support which allowed me to get it all out in my own time, acknowledged and respected everything I was feeling helped me to regain a sense of perspective and ability to move back towards coping. Sometimes we are not coping and that is allowed.

120: Talked to, and more importantly listened to, several people both established and new at the HOSS on a day when the Highland weather was so dismal it was making every trouble seem worse, yet there was a sense of joy and lighter load from sharing and just being together in a safe, understanding place.

I have spent a lot of time yearning to be able to let myself relax and listen more but being terrified of being branded quiet or shy. It is so frustrating explaining over and over again that I do have things to say but I am tired, anxious and the conversation has inevitably moved on by the time I examined whatever I wanted to say for faux pas potential. Or, indeed, I was interested in what others were saying and enjoying listening to it! I wish that society could just forget about labelling people quiet or shy and get it into the collective psyche that to be an interesting person, you need to be an interested person.

121: Reading a very interesting, surreal comic fantasy novel with elements of science fiction. It is a wonderful, "all you can think buffet" of futuristic ideas and I especially loved reading about the transport system involving freefall through the Earth from London to Sydney.

This refers to the "Thursday Next" fantasy detective novels by Jasper Fforde. These novels are a real find; a combination of science fiction and surrealism, allusions to the classics, sophisticated word play and humour which ranges from the complex and intellectual through situation comedy all the way to outright slapstick. At the same time there are surprisingly poignant storylines and the odd unexpectedly powerful psychological impact comes out of nowhere. They got me re-reading some classics. The series must be read in chronological order to get the most out of it.

122: Looking at the webcam of a cruise ship where a friend is on holiday has been a fascinating and comforting experience. I always feel the separation when she is out of the UK as she is the friend with whom I tend to communicate in most detail but I always give her space when she is on holiday. Seeing the ship gives structure to her absence and makes me happy for her.

Coping when our usual sources of support are away is an important part of managing our lives. Part of this is trying not to become reliant on one person; this isn't healthy for either party. There may well end up being one person we talk to more than anyone else, or tell more details to than anyone else, but it is important to have other support there and to have coping skills for times we have to wait.

123: Feeling satisfied with a full day's work on three different projects but also with having known when to stop, leaving myself time to have a relaxing evening, a decent dinner and unwind. So often I push myself too hard and lose subsequent days to headaches and fatigue.

Intense focus and loss of awareness can prevent us from looking after ourselves and have a bad effect on us in the long run. Estelle Ryan's remarkable Connection series, about the loss adjuster turned detective Dr Genevieve Lenard, features examples of this as part of Dr Lenard's autism. Her personal journey can be heartwrenching to read as she is forced to let others move into her personal space for security reasons. The insight into her complex character and autism including meltdowns is intricately and sensitively handled. Very absorbing novels.

124: Out in pre-Springtime sunshine today reflecting on a successful week at work and socially, I felt a rare, genuine high for the first time in a while. My energy levels were raised and I gave thanks in my mind over and over again, wanting to capture and commit the feeling to memory.

It is good to acknowledge our steps forward, though we should not be conditioned to only feel happy when we have succeeded. It is ableist to exclusively link a person's value to their successes, including our own value. The pre-Springtime sunshine alone was a good reason to feel joy.

125: Doing work on an autism library database has been so interesting and encouraging, seeing just how much help and guidance and shared experience is out there on a wide range of topics. The guidance is as much to help non-autistic people meet us halfway as to guide us!

The autistic voice needs to be boosted and encouraged as the key source of expertise on autism. This needs to include all types of communication and especially the less heard autistic people. Intersectionality is where people are in more than one marginalised group, such as disabled people in ethnic minorities and / or with diverse gender identities. Many are living in poverty without access to the resources to reach an audience. I am lucky in many respects and I recognise that this is privilege. I would like to ask anyone reading this to consider doing an online search using terms such as "writing by black autistic women" and "writing by transgender autistic people"; please support them.

126: I was given a beautiful, colourful plant today as a thankyou for spending three hours doing a task I thoroughly enjoyed. My colleagues had been dreading it as it was very repetitive and precise, but it was ideal for me as I found it relaxing and rewarding; a win win situation.

This is another example of autism as an asset to the workplace, whether we can manage to work full time, part time or volunteer for a couple of hours a week.

127: I was wondering today, what would I do differently if I were not autistic, and of course I cannot speak from experience as nobody gets to be both autistic and non-autistic so I cannot ever know how it would feel to make choices from that perspective. However, I could not think of any principle or routine I would want to change.

Nobody gets to be both. That is a simple truth with a hint of sadness as there is so much desire to understand on both sides. We do, however, have many features in common; autism is amplified experience, not opposite experience, in many ways. Sensory overload is an example of this. Often this excess of experience causes us problems. Yet we share so many of our needs and goals.

128: Lovely time with much missed group of colleagues who are also my dear friends. After an extra long meeting, there was much talk of dancing in the aisle on the train home. When it came to the moment, my sophisticated and attractive colleagues admitted they were too timid; I gave them a twirl and made it an impromptu onboard party.

I have had a few moments like that over the years; often on trains, sometimes compensating for less uplifting moments on the journey. On a recent journey back to Nairn after my weekly visit to Aviemore which involves two trains each way, I first had a scare when there was nobody manning the automatic ticket barriers at Inverness as they do not open for through tickets and then the mortification of returning a hello from a complete stranger, having mistakenly thought it was directed to me. I often do not recognise casual acquaintances out of context due to my face blindness so if someone says hello in passing, I will answer rather than risk offence. When I then have to sit in fairly close proximity as the person to whom they were actually speaking appears from behind me and a long, lively conversation ensues, it feels soul destroying. Luckily on this occasion the full moon was rising in a beautiful clear evening sky and I distracted myself taking photos; the moon is always a source of comfort to me. As the guard came through checking tickets, he saw the photo I had just taken and I pointed out the real thing through the carriage window; he admired it then said jokingly that it wasn't a good sign, presumably in tongue in cheek anticipation of lively passengers as the train continued on its two hour journey to Aberdeen. It says a lot about autistic impulsiveness as well as my liking for being unconventional that I had no reservations whatsoever about doing a werewolf howl. To me that was far less embarrassing than having appeared desperate by saying hello to someone who wasn't intending to greet me.

129: Yet another "I saw you..." conversation in a shop, which normally I hate and find very uncomfortable as I am at a disadvantage with my tendency not to register people when I don't expect to see them and I don't like the feeling that people know my business, turned into a joyous sharing of interest as I had been in my garden sat out for the first time this year writing to a penpal, a rare tradition.

The only drawback of living in a relatively small town for me is the high incidence of being seen by people and then hearing about it afterwards. I find it intrusive and it makes it difficult to relax, feeling that I am on display. In Aviemore I had bus drivers ask me why I didn't get on nearer to where I live; I walked into a restaurant bar and was related a chronological list of the last few sightings. I had a local taxi driver chase after me in Inverness to give me his card in case I ever missed my train as he had seen me and he worked in both places; ironically I was rushing for a train at the time. Fair play to an honest grafter for showing initiative in building up his business but I do sometimes feel as though I'm on Big Brother. I have always been a very fast walker, which is good as it allows me to incorporate healthy exercise into my routine but that draws even more attention to me. If I had a pound for every time someone has told me I look / looked as though I were on a mission, I wouldn't need to be writing this book as I would already have raised thousands. The I Saw Yous can be very oppressive as there is no way of switching them off when I need my space and solitude but they do sometimes lead to pleasant and friendly conversation. My first I Saw You instance in Nairn was unusual in that for once, the other person was mistaken. I knew for a fact that I had not been in the specified place at the specified time. Still in the extra fatigued stage of recovering from my house move weeks earlier, I had not even been out of bed. I felt slightly mean spirited for being glad that a well meaning, friendly neighbour, who has shown me nothing but courtesy and respect, was mistaken! It just felt so good to be vindicated for once and let off the "here we go again" round of embarrassment, frustration and guilt at having inadvertently snubbed someone!

130: It is always disappointing waking up to overcast skies after a bluebird day which was supposed to be followed by more of the same, but how uplifting to see the passing Highland Chieftain which manages to draw upon every available atom of light and turn pearlescent, silver and white carriages glowing. I always get inspiration and energy when I need it from my beloved train.

Of course I do not always believe everything I am told (another of the sweeping and inaccurate stereotypes which some hold about autistic people), including the weather forecast! There is a difference between wanting to believe something and believing it without question. If the weather forecast is good, I will want to believe it; if it is bad, I will tell myself it's probably wrong! I do not imagine for a moment that this is exclusive to me, or to autistic people! "Bluebird days" is a name given to cloudless, brilliantly sharp days with crisp air and powdered snow on the mountains, especially by the snowsports community. They are rare and special; the air has a certain quality which can cut through layers of fatigue. They feel different from the moment of waking.

131: A friendly chat with a delivery man about TV listings and football on the big screen made me feel better on a day I was low, stressed and very fragile. Small talk and nothing to do with my particular interests, but it helped; stereotypes about autism do not always hold.

Small talk. We can do it; we sometimes choose to do it. Sometimes it annoys us or seems irrelevant but it isn't taboo throughout the entire autistic community! Neither do we always have the same tolerance or capacity for it. Just because we can and want to engage in it on some occasions does not mean that the times we are not up for it are any less authentic. Some autistic people find it hard to imagine why so many people want to make small talk about the weather. One of the best solidarity moments I ever had at an event was when one of the other autistic people there pointed out that weather chitchat is not only accepted but expected whereas he gets questioning looks if he mentions his interest in cloud formations. So much this, as we say to show enthusiastic agreement on social media these days! Personally, I don't mind weather chatter. What I rail against is the ritualistic "How are you" conversation when there is only one permissible type of answer, especially if on a bad day that answer is not given convincingly enough and attracts a telling off in the name of banter! It is isolating for people when they really are not fine, being forced to pretend to be. Autistic people do tend to find it difficult to lie and are often very private. We know it's not appropriate to go into detail about not being fine to someone who is just selling us a newspaper or delivering our shopping order. We don't particularly want to tell them all about it either. Being forced to say we're fine and be convincing about it on our worst days is beyond the obligations of civility and a stage too far. I have been known to suggest to people that if they want Mary Poppins, they should buy the DVD.

132: I had to tap into reserves of strength today that I didn't know I had, as I had to go to a big meeting in a hot, crowded room on a day when I was already low and overloaded, then was immediately put in the situation of having to respond to some negative remarks about a colleague who was also present and is transgender. Somehow I found words to defend her there and then. In the formal meeting I sat next to someone interested in autism who was excited about the HOSS then I was told I had an air of enjoying everything I do, so I guess I coped!

Autistic people tend to have a very strong sense of justice and many feel immense solidarity with other minority groups, making it intolerable for us when we encounter prejudice. Some people, including some autistic people tend to compartmentalise and see one minority or disability at a time; they struggle with the realisation that someone can for instance be autistic and use a wheelchair, or be disabled and gay. Intersectionality and privilege are concepts which evoke a lot of strong emotion but need to be respectfully acknowledged in order to build an inclusive society. Fear and ignorance have much to answer for; so much can be achieved by listening to other minorities, amplifying their voices and fully accepting that being in any particular minority does not give us the right to try to speak over those who have experienced things we never will. I was astonished when I was told at the meeting that day about having an air of enjoying everything I do; I was forcing it so much that day, I must have overcompensated more than I realised!

133: Feeling stressed about a complicated work situation, it simultaneously occurred to me that I used to come to the Highlands to get away from this sort of thing and that I experience it here now because my life is up here and I wouldn't have it any other way. That response to autism-heightened stress is an even stronger bond than good times.

The first real test of being up here full time started so innocuously. Someone waved to me as she drove past me shortly after I moved here and as she had the same colour hair and same coloured car as a friend of my neighbour, I thought in that fleeting moment that it was this friend and waved back. Throughout that summer, this person and her friends waved and tooted at me every time they saw me when driving around the village; because of my face blindness, although by this time I realised I had been mistaken about who I first thought it was, I assumed I must be known to them from somewhere local and just not recognising them out of context. However they became increasingly mocking and I became very uneasy every time I went out, even though they weren't doing anything drastic. I was deeply ashamed of having been targeted, especially as well meaning friends told me there must be something about my demeanour that marked me out as a victim. I was involved in the initial stages of planning the HOSS, still trying to establish myself and earn respect as a colleague and collaborator, unable to tell the people in that part of my life what was happening. I had stopped waving back at these people and my neighbour wanted me to involve the police but I felt it would be unreasonable when I had been waving back for quite a few weeks. I started to keep a record of when it was happening and eventually I saw the car stopped in the street with the group sitting in it. As they had never been threatening, only mildly mocking in their behaviour and there were other people around, I went to ask them where I knew them from. The blonde lady who had started it all admitted that they didn't know me at all but had just seen me one day and decided to wave at me then continued doing it because I had waved back. I laughed and walked away; it tailed off after that but it was a long time before I could relax and it still has a legacy today because I am very reluctant to respond to any greetings from a car unless I know the car or can see who it is (not always easy with the light on slanting windows) so it has added to the I Saw You dilemma! I wish I knew why they chose to wave at me in the first place but I am glad I knew better than to ask; it would have given them power and I may have found it difficult to cope with the answer. I refuse to be blamed; it started as a simple mistaken identity and I did nothing wrong. Even if I acted in an eccentric way, it wouldn't be right to target me for it but I would at least have the option to make an informed choice to either acknowledge that some people will choose to be bullies and deal with it, or hold back on any quirks if I wanted a quiet life. All I was doing was walking around the place, presumably looking happy! It hurt to have something like this happen to me up here especially so soon, but I never expected my problems to go away because of where I live, no matter how much I love it. The crucial fact is, it did not devalue my life here.

134: Blessed today with the gift beyond price of a stunningly scenic journey on the proud and mighty Highland Chieftain with sun and blue skies from the border, rose gold sunset from horizon to horizon via the inside of the carriages between Stirling and Pitlochry, then a dark rainbow of twilight on old snow over Druimuachdar and a starry Highland homecoming sky.

Here is why the euphoria always returns. I have twice in all my travels, once on the Highland Chieftain and once on ScotRail, been travelling south between Inverness and Aviemore and seen the stunning spectacle of moonlit monochrome on one side of the train and multicoloured dawn or sunset on the other. I have twice seen a dark red sunrise; once passing Culloden Moor, which was spine tingling. We are blessed.

135: Good news of the ospreys returning to Scotland for the new season. People follow news of their nests online and often ascribe human emotions to them, but it is refreshing to get away from all that nuanced complexity and just follow what happens in nature; straightforward survival and self sufficiency!

It can be annoying to read the comments on the blogs where people insist on talking about the ospreys as though they were people and turning it into yet another example of conformist society. There are plenty of places where people can read gossip about celebrities and sex. Of course the analogies can be funny but they go too far as people get carried away and have arguments. They're ospreys. Not people. End of!

136: Two years ago today I got on the Highland Chieftain with a one way ticket, making my longed for move to the Highlands after 25 years. This year the anniversary coincides with the clocks going forward; I also celebrate the hour change (both ways) for the freshness it gives the daily routine, without having to do anything different. So it feels like a double celebration and chance to take stock and anticipate.

One of my quirks of which I am proudest is that I always celebrate the changing of the clocks, in both directions. I have loved the ritual from childhood; the sense of novelty it gives to the daily and weekly routine. I remember as a very young child my mother telling me on our Sunday visit to my grandparents that next week it would be dark when we came home; I wondered how she knew. It was an early example of my tendency to internalise quickly but process and respond slowly that I absorbed the mystery of that throwaway comment but didn't ask her. Many autistic people, especially children, struggle with the sudden change to their everyday environment when the clocks change. I understand; I realise I am very lucky to be able to enjoy it so much and wish I could give them the gift of getting the same joy from it.

137: World Autism Acceptance Day and the first birthday of the HOSS; a special day by all accounts but for me it was once in a lifetime, engraved on my heart forever special; a potent psychological cocktail of seeing many friends, facing intense fears, breaking down barriers which time and circumstances created between me and hero-worshipped colleagues, and sunlit train journeys: unforgettable.

I will never forget, even though some of those barriers go up and down periodically. It is important to have a tangible reminder of days like that; write about them while the memories are fresh, keep any photos. It's like looking at someone else at times.

138: Dealing with a phase of insomnia, I have managed to start a day feeling good as I got up very early and read through some of my correspondence and coping strategies built up with the HOSS. It is such a blessing that its ongoing presence and support can benefit me not just in business hours but at yet another misty 5am.

We so often need support at inconvenient times; a lot of the time this will mean friends and family, carers or supporting ourselves. The Internet is a blessing at these times, providing it is used safely; we must always remember when we are feeling vulnerable that people we only know casually online may not be who they say they are or have genuine motives. Just like in other aspects of life, online friendships can turn out to be deeply rewarding, even lifesaving. At the same time, they have to be built up gradually over time and trust has to be established in an informed way. It is never a good idea to give too much away online where it may be read by more people than we are aware of and can trust. Distracting ourselves with an interest is a useful way to get by until we can access trusted support.

139: Watching the sleeper to Euston swish by in a string of soft, soothing lights embodied the gentle spirit of a Sunday night with the journey of rest and recharging into the life and connections and business of a new week; an immediate need for peace and solitude combined with a longing for useful, productive interaction.

Our needs so often appear to contradict each other. I yearn equally for contact and solitude. The right balance is elusive and ever changing.

140: Struggling on my own with a computer upgrade, my technical knowledge limited and my usual source of IT help away, I discovered a further upgrade was needed just to be able to keep going online and do everything else. I was so stressed, the darkness of a shutdown was descending as the task ahead was so huge and unfamiliar yet vital to my routine. I forced myself to make a phone call, had a nice chat and got my upgrade free and payments halved!

I had waited far too long as I didn't have the time or the energy to deal with the change and of course eventually I had no choice. It kept me indoors with stress and overload throughout the sunniest Easter weekend I have ever known. I got there in the end and I learned the practical lesson that ongoing subscriptions rather than one-off purchases would give me access to a more suitable system of gradual small updates.

141: Another good session at the HOSS with friends old and new. It made me evaluate my feelings about friendship and my need to instinctively compete to "keep" people; my friends' very different personalities and viewpoints and relationships (or not!) to each other while they still mean so much to me individually, help me to realise that people can have multiple strong bonds.

I still struggle to get my head around the fact that friends and colleagues can have close relationships with and immensely high regard for other people without it diverting anything away from their relationship to me. There are two people in particular connected to my work with the HOSS who are especially close to my heart (King's Cross to Inverness, you know who you are). I know that neither of them, cherished as they are, takes anything away from what the other means to me. Applying that knowledge to let myself trust in friendships and working partnerships I share with much higher achievers is a work in progress; these two make it feasible.

142: Got a very heartfelt and encouraging "Well done" from a friend who is not autistic, when I told her about a practical change I had to deal with. I hadn't expected her to appreciate as much as she did how difficult it had been for me. This understanding has been made possible by the HOSS helping me to meet the world halfway.

This may be an unpopular view among people who are justifiably drained and depleted by explaining things over and over but we do need to educate and cannot expect people just to know. There is a lot of information available to anyone who genuinely seeks out autistic and other disabled input; we can all help ourselves and others by looking something up instead of bombarding disabled people who are exhausted and in pain with questions. Sometimes a genuine query coming from an authentic desire to understand and learn from a conflict can be just too much at that time and provoke a harsh reply. I have seen many bitter arguments erupt on social media. The option is always there to back off and either do a bit of research (if, for instance, a word or expression used has caused a problem) or wait until emotions are no longer running high. Among the people in our daily lives, we need to be prepared to help them when they want to understand and do better by us; the key to that is in first understanding ourselves. It is surprising how much easier it can be to put words to our own experience when we recognise the common threads in the experiences of others.

143: As part of a computer upgrade I finally deleted a file I had kept for eight years to remind me of a time in my life when, not yet diagnosed autistic, I ended up in a situation I handled badly and had to defend myself at work with a detailed statement. I will never forget or forgive myself, but with the support of the HOSS I could take the step of deleting the file.

I truly could not imagine a way forward from that time. After 18 months of assorted counselling type arrangements, crisis visits to my GP and work medicals in harsh, draining beige and grey rooms, I was finally referred for autism assessment. From there I came to Number 6 in Edinburgh and four years later made my dream move to the Highlands at the time the HOSS was being planned.

144: Dealt with a noisy office environment, a busy train with more loud noise, a very fast paced group session and finding my way around unfamiliar accommodation, plus a very busy supermarket and a disappointing short notice cancellation; all in one day. Yet I am happy and relaxed, thanks to warm conversation at the HOSS.

A day like that could so easily have gone the other way and taken me months or years to recover from. How blessed we are to have informed services, removing the need to explain our complex difficulties when so overloaded we are shutting down and can hardly speak.

145: A beautifully sunny Easter Day; a festival that means so much to people for many different reasons, religious or secular and is marked in so many different ways. At the same time it is not as built up, all pervading and routine suspending as Christmas! A more autism friendly holiday in many ways; a blank canvas for a personal commemoration.

We often hear about Christmas being in the summer in the southern hemisphere but rarely about their Easter being in the autumn. It is a fascinating concept; I love the renewal of Springtime but I also feel a strong sense of new life and reawakenings in the autumn, as the air freshens and the colours erupt from all the green.

146: Allowed myself to ask for help from a friend with something that is in his line of work. It was hard to overcome both my pride and my reluctance to bother people but I had done as much as I could on my own. It was a load off my mind, I learned some useful tips and he was complimentary about how far I got on my own; he even learned a couple of things too.

Asking for help is very difficult for me and it is not just down to pride. I always have a fear that the more I ask for help, the less independent I will be and the more social energy I will have to use. Something I have learned from discussions at the HOSS in recent years is the difference between independence and autonomy; the latter is what is really important. We can all need varying amounts of help and still have choices, input and decision making power in our own lives.

147: A stressful phone call became a pleasure when the operator renewing my Railcard said it had already been sent out yesterday after initially being printed upside down, then realised she was looking at last year. I said it was impressive value for money getting a third off time travel as well and it made us both keep going off into fits of giggles, making a much better start to the day.

I so often experience the frustration of not thinking of what I should have said until after the event; my autism heightens these feelings. Creative writing can be an excellent outlet and it is exciting that we have a growing creative writing group now at the HOSS, created and led by one of our own.

148: Excellent sensory experience today, went over to pet a cat on my way to the shop and two more appeared from nowhere as cats do and ran up to me. I can still feel all that fur and see all their colours and pretty markings and hear their chatty miaows and purrs. Worth being the local cat lady!

Stereotypes can be intersectional too. As a single woman who loves cats and uses spectacles, I refused to be called a librarian when that was part of my volunteering! Libraries are much more vibrant community hubs now; I have to admit I preferred them as places of refuge with their hushed atmosphere and the smell of books.

149: The air is lovely and soft today; in the adult diagnosis group this week the subject was sensory issues and one of the things we talked about was how many of us love the night time as we can feel the different, softer texture of the air. A very upbeat, positive theme to carry with us into everyday life and appreciate more.

I love the uncluttered night hours. Modern life channels us to pack more and more into the day and live according to timetables which have nothing to do with nature or, crucially, with our sensory needs. Preferring the night gives me a feeling of rebelliousness, "playing along" with the expectations of the daytime. I love to see a sundial lit by the moon; it represents a life lived out of sync with established conventions and routines. The silver light originates from the same source as through the day, our life giving sun, but diverted around a complex world into a realm of senses on recharge before reaching the sundial. It reflects but doesn't give the reading it is intended to. All the world can expect of a sundial overnight is just to be.

150: Ejected a wasp from the HOSS kitchen today. I am scared of them but other people there were even more so and for good reason. Told it as I swept it out of the window that it was taking liberties and needed to literally buzz off. I don't feel quite so afraid of them now.

A professional was one of the people who was scared, having seen a family member get stung during their childhood. A culture of hierarchy would see many professionals horrified to find themselves in a position of being helped by a service user. That was definitely not the case in this situation.

Rainbow alongside the Highland Chieftain,
Aviemore

151: There was a rainbow right over the Highland Chieftain at Aviemore yesterday evening, the curve exactly following the outline of the engine, with one of the station lights in between. People are telling me I should enter the photo I took in competitions as I notice and capture such images, especially my favourite subjects!

I love rainbows, especially rare variants; multiple bows, moonbows etc. I have often seen them at significant times and on special days. I also love to look at them, knowing many people associate them and others' appreciation of them with unworldly and excessive optimism whilst I am actually wondering just how indigo got in there when it is so dark. That is my favourite part of the visible spectrum; a tribute to the soft, soothing peace of the night amid the daytime sky at its brightest.

152: A dear friend received an award for her work for our fellow autistic people in the Highlands and beyond. This is a proud and happy time, to see her efforts justly rewarded and the achievement going towards the ongoing quest to show the positive, empathic face of autism to educate the wider community.

Big time respect, KB: I have learned so much.

153: Staying in a friend's house, I had been preparing myself to watch TV shows with her which I wouldn't normally because I associate them with past environments before my diagnosis when I didn't fit in with the office "water cooler gossip" culture but didn't know why. On one show, two boys sang a song they wrote about bullying and received a prolonged standing ovation. I am glad I was privileged to see its debut.

We should not make ourselves avoid something we may enjoy just because it seems to be what everyone else is doing. If we do, we are as guilty of being influenced by the crowd as we would be if we embraced it purely because everyone else did. We should always guard against closing our minds.

154: Another day of holiday related upheaval, involving a worrying wait for someone who was very late to meet me and didn't hear her phone, then another new place to find and negotiate the entry system. So rewarding to get inside, shoes off, slippers on and discover a very Gothic raised snug / dining area and a wonderful green velvet pear doorstop to use as a sensory object – so apt to soothe after things went pear-shaped!

I was helping out at a very successful autism conference straight after that holiday and spent a lot of time holding onto the petty cash box to keep it safe and easily accessible when needed. It meant one thing fewer for the organisers, who had worked phenomenally hard, to worry about. I liked the texture of the box and it was quite comforting to have something solid to hold on a day when I was quite nervous about getting my contribution just right. I told quite a few people it was my sensory object for the day; I was half joking, though I suspect some may have taken me literally. It's like the blanket special interests stereotype; there are degrees of significance to sensory objects. Some are simply an enjoyable bonus at a particular time and place. It's a gift to be able to appreciate things in a different way; I feel lucky to perceive it.

155: Out for lunch with my brother, both of us having hot meals, I was moaning to him that I was the only one of us to get the very obvious and therefore insulting "Watch, the plate's hot" warning; the subtle, indefinable differentness of autism is sadly often mistaken for lack of any autonomy, awareness or common sense. My brother restored my perspective by pointing out his plate wasn't hot. At the same time, he took my feelings seriously.

I'm sure it isn't unique to autistic people and a lot of it is to do with compensation culture but we tend to attract the most ridiculous and pointless warnings at times. It's one of the drawbacks of winter for me; when the pavements are icy, I wear suitable footwear, focus on every step and get on with my life just like everyone else but complete strangers feel the need to tell me to be careful. What more can I do; I'm already visibly making my way along with appropriate caution just as they are! It is one of the most difficult aspects of facing the world every day on my own with no moral support or backing available in the moment. My brother Matthew (not a biological brother; my best friend) is the only one who can reach me when my self esteem is at its lowest and make me believe I may just possibly be taking it too far. Part of that is taking my feelings seriously; not dismissing them, acknowledging how real they are to me and presenting a reasoned and genuine alternative. Matthew knows, without ever having had to be prompted, not to add unhelpful pressure and guilt by telling me that people are Trying To Be Nice. Most of the time they probably are, but it is deeply ingrained into my psyche to feel that they are trying to score points. I am working on accepting that this instinct is a permanent part of me and what I can and must control is how I react. The people who can help me with that are the ones who come from a standpoint of taking my feelings seriously and respecting the intensity and effect of those feelings, even if they do not agree. They also need to appreciate it when my autistic logic comes out and I point out things like the potential for someone already concentrating on the ice to fall when distracted by someone shouting a superflous warning! Seriously. Everyone reading this who knows me will be chuckling to themselves at this part because they all know what I'm like when I get started on this subject. Beyond the laughter, though, it genuinely is something which causes me a lot of anguish and frustration. I cannot and will not presume to say how other autistic people should feel, but we are trying. Believe me, whenever we Do It Again, whether it is saying the wrong thing, bumping into a doorframe, catching a foot on a threshold or slopping a cup of tea, we know. Chances are we didn't want to do it and were already doing our best to avoid it, we may well be vexed that it happened yet again and mortified that you saw it. We don't need you to tell us to watch out; we thought we were. We don't need an infantilising "Oops!" or a loud squeal as if to make sure nobody else round about missed it. If we vocalised every time somebody messed up it would be pathologised as autistic indiscretion!

156: Decided to start a food diary to help me stop my weight gain and tendency to overeat to make up for other things which are missing from my life. It is a constructive way to use my autistic honesty as I know I will be strict about recording everything even just for my own reference and it will deter me from making unhealthy choices.

Using autistic traits to our advantage is one of the best skills we can develop. When it comes to dieting, though, we also have to watch for our tendency to become obsessively focused. I made sure that the emphasis remained on healthy choices, not trying to eat less and less, and that I allowed for enough treats to keep my metabolism guessing (otherwise it slows down into starvation mode and stores more fat). Serious dieting for significant weight loss should always be monitored by a doctor or dietician.

157: Today is the Highland Chieftain's official 30th birthday. It is a very special day for a special interest and I am so proud of the magnificent old girl. I am also very grateful to have so many people – mostly connected to the HOSS – in my life who appreciate what my train means to me and never bat an eyelid at my referring to an InterCity 125 as my BFF or my baby.

She's an equal opportunities Chieftain of course! The year before, I marked her birthday at the HOSS. It was a revelation to find myself so unquestioningly understood when I told people what I was celebrating. I had brought in some gluten free shortbread and when I took it out of my bag, my ticket for my ScotRail journey in from Aviemore (the Chieftain gets into Inverness in the evening so I have to use the local trains for day trips) was bizarrely stuck to the box. Everyone appreciated the random humour in this too. How refreshing to have the option of celebrating such unconventional, personal milestones with other people.

The Highland Chieftain at Inverness

158: At a much anticipated and long planned event for autistic people, a speaker made a huge and very brave personal revelation (not about their autism, but they are autistic). The way the whole room silently came together in acceptance and support was an unforgettable moment of a lifetime and made a complete nonsense of any perception that all autistic people lack empathy.

It was a moment I can still feel; the atmosphere intensified and I could sense it recording itself indelibly into the memories of everyone there. Autistic people do have empathy; sometimes more than is good for us as we feel too much.

159: On a day when I felt so bad I plummeted back into an agoraphobic and practically non-verbal shutdown state, I received an email opportunity to participate in a research survey on autism in schools; my schooldays were a long time ago but I found myself able to remember and express opinions in a style which had seemed to be lost to me; I still have a voice.

Accessible participation in our own time; processing and editing what we want to say is essential for us to be able to give feedback. So is having a safe space to deal with whatever feelings and memories are stirred up, whether at an event or participating from home.

160: Bought a lovely cheery solar light for the garden; a tall yellow flower. Looking out of the window at dusk waiting to see it come on for the first time is a gently stimulating end to another day of mental ill health. I bought the light when out for a walk which I forced myself to take to fight a descent into agoraphobia.

It was a very difficult walk to take even through the peaceful streets of my then home town I loved so much; I had to do it because the longer I'd left it, the harder it would have been to leave the house. We all have bad days and need to allow for that but cannot let avoidance get a grip on us. I love my yellow rose; a constant reminder not to give in. I do not have a garden in Nairn but my rose is still with me as an indoor light on a sunny windowsill.

The rose light in my garden in Aviemore

161: Experiences described by others in a group at the HOSS resonated strongly with a current bad mental health crisis I am experiencing. It is awful to think of others feeling what I am feeling right now, yet at the same time it helps me feel less alone and less dysfunctional and it gives me added incentive to get through the low and help others.

I have a particular event in my life which I use as a marker when my mental health dips; that I need to get back to a state where I was strong enough to give the situation the outcome I did. It will come as no surprise to anyone by this point that it's a train story and involves the Highland Chieftain. I unavoidably overheard the conversation when the lady at the table in front of me had her ticket checked; she had made a last minute change to her plans late the previous night as she already had a flight booked days later but needed to get to London urgently due to a family emergency. Unfortunately, being unfamiliar with the online ticket purchasing procedures, she hadn't realised that she needed to collect her ticket from the station and thought that the printout she had was all she needed on the train. The guard, who was very sympathetic but sticking to the rules, had reluctantly told her she would have to get off the train at Edinburgh and either get her ticket from the machine there or go to the travel centre if the machine there wouldn't issue it, then get on the next train to London. Upset, she had to phone her family and tell them, then get her luggage together. I was getting off at Edinburgh Waverley and knew that with my knowledge of this station, there was a chance I could take her to the machines, grab a member of staff to get her ticket and see her back on board the Chieftain which was due to sit at Waverley for 15 minutes before going onwards to London. The next train had a lot more stops and was notorious for being very busy; it would also have meant she arrived in London at the start of rush hour. It took all the strength and courage I could muster as quite apart from approaching an already stressed stranger, I had to admit to having listened to something which wasn't my business, albeit with a view to helping. I was also getting into this situation with no guarantee of success; I couldn't be certain of getting her ticket sorted in time to get her back on board the Chieftain. I told her that I had been sitting right behind her and couldn't help hearing her situation and as I lived locally and knew the station well, I would show her where to go and help her get her ticket. Waverley Station was especially complicated to navigate at that time as it was in the midst of major refurbishment. She accepted my help, not having been in the station for years and I was prepared to take her right to the front of a queue if necessary, telling anyone I had to that it was an emergency. As it happened, there was no queue and one of the staff was there to help with the ticket; I got her back on the Chieftain with a few minutes to spare. I will never know what happened with her family but I do know from looking at the East Coast website later that day that the Chieftain was the last train to get through Peterborough before a major signal failure. If that poor woman had been on the next train, she would have had the stress of it stopping and the announcements about being delayed for an unknown time, then after 20 extra minutes she would have arrived into London in the very heart of the rush hour. The Chieftain got into King's Cross several minutes early.

162: Loving the feeling of accomplishment on a Friday evening when I've gotten things done; following my routine in general helps me to preserve favourite times of the week, having them to look forward to and enjoy when they come around each time. It keeps my life from becoming chaotic when I am struggling.

I had a lovely conversation with a close colleague about this. It is so important to keep the weekends distinct and special, not only for autistic people but for anyone facing redundancy or retirement or any other situation where all the days become the same. Even something as simple as having instant coffee through the week and a cafetiere at the weekend helps to give that structure and variety. With my fatigue issues I spread my housework across the week and that leads to the "Friday feeling" people talk about. It doesn't have to follow the traditional Saturday and Sunday weekend pattern either; each individual will have their own favourite days.

163: Catching up with reruns of an old favourite TV show, Third Rock from the Sun, about aliens coming to Earth disguised as people and having to fit in in order to research the planet. It is hilarious and very feelgood but it also echoes the dilemma faced by autistic people every day as we try to fit into a world where we don't have the perspective we're expected to and can appear to. It is exaggerated for comic effect but sometimes not so far from our reality! It is good to be reminded to see the funny side.

The characters have to learn human emotions and social rules while concealing the fact they are different. My favourite part of the show is when they are sitting out on a rooftop under the window of the fabulous attic apartment they live in, surrounded by an eclectic variety of outdoor fairy lights and discussing the events of the episode.

164: There was a brief spell of thunder and lightning today. I love the way the air becomes charged and the earth seems to be holding its breath; a bit like how it feels to be about to walk into a social situation! Then it's bright light, a lot of noise and counting the seconds until the atmosphere relaxes!

It can feel like this every time an autistic person walks into any social or group setting. There is the tension, that suffocating feeling of the air we are trying to breathe, that foreboding crackle of potential flashpoint and then the sensory flare of walking into the situation. Knowing that others feel the same is such a relief.

165: Had a referral made from the HOSS team. It involved a lot of very indepth and tiring questions but it was handled so sensitively, it showed just how important it is to have autism specific services. I was even able to attend a group afterwards, which I rarely have the energy to do after an appointment of that nature.

This is a major benefit of the HOSS and all the one stop shops. Appointments of that nature are tiring for anyone but especially for autistic people who find all interaction demanding on our energy levels. I was very fortunate to be in such an understanding and informed setting where I was able to set the pace and answer in my own time. Thank you KS.

166: Tidying the garden on the first sunny day in ages was very therapeutic and gave me a sense of achievement and control of managing my environment. Mitzi knew just when I needed to be encouraged to take a break, coming over from her own garden across the road and distracting me to pet her; I will take such guidance from a cat quicker than from a person!

Animals are so empathic. This is no myth; they really do know.

167: Feeling immense satisfaction looking out at my latest set of solar lights in the garden as the sun charges them up. Bought for £1.50 each as basic white lights, all it took was a few strips of coloured cellophane to turn one light purple, one orange and one turquoise. I have more than one favourite colour (especially for lights) and more than one special interest!

I have already mentioned special interests in that talking enthusiastically about something doesn't automatically make it a "special interest" or obsession or whatever people choose to call them! Where is the line between regular interest and special interest anyway, I wonder, and as long as it's safe, legal and not interfering with health, hygiene, nutrition and the quality of the rest of a person's life, does it matter? A bit of creativity can add so much to life and one of the many blessings of autism is when logical thinking combines with impulsiveness to have and act on such ideas.

168: Reading some very good articles online about introverts and extroverts gave me a lot of food for thought; it is not only autism itself and associated conditions which need some serious stereotype busting but also non medical, personality related characteristics. I have some of the introvert characteristics but also many of the extrovert ones. The key revealing insight was tying it in with people's energy, not personality!

Finally, someone gets it!!! I cannot quote the article itself in case of copyright violation but the general gist was that whether someone is predominantly introvert or extrovert is dictated by where they get their energy from. Extroverts draw energy from the noise and buzz of interacting with groups of people and use it up dealing with the times they are on their own, whereas introverts use their energy in dealing with the stimuli and need to recharge in their alone time. Nothing to do with how much personality they have, how much they have to say, how interesting they are, their goodwill towards others, their effort or even necessarily their confidence. A lot of damage is done by society's insistence on labelling and categorising people; further anguish is caused by not acknowledging that these so called characteristics can fluctuate. There are pockets of insight and connection out there in all that chaos.

169: A small and specific positive landmark on a day which is a poignant anniversary of my only face to face meeting with a former work contact I revered; a day when I always feel very vulnerable about my limited social life and lack of closeness and reciprocity in my life. It fell on Thursday when I always get a text around 1pm about my shopping delivery. On any Thursday I get annoyed when I forget to expect it and feel excited that someone text me. Today, I remembered but it was only one of four texts, the others from friends.

The worst time was when I was waiting for a friend and her children who as it turned out got all of my texts at once hours later, holding the biggest table in an increasingly busy pub. When a text came through at 1pm I was immensely relieved; well and truly caught out as it was of course the delivery related one. It's amazing the significance that text and remembering to expect it has taken on in my life; recently the time it comes through has started to vary, which makes it worse. As for that acquaintance of long ago, it is a sad truth that some charismatic people who appear to shine the light of goodness and compassion so brightly are hiding a fear governed response to any form of diversity which as soon as it brushes against their personal lives propels them by some arcane reflex straight back to the dark ages. This includes autism, which I didn't then know I had, and mental health issues, which I did. The day I met her was in many ways the beginning of a journey which would lead to my diagnosis, via some very dark places. It also brought me the gift of one of my best friends, whose faith in me started strong in unlikely circumstances and has never faltered; Gabi, again and always I thank you.

170: Enjoyed a lively, convivial group chat at the HOSS on a day which is a personal celebration. I was made to feel very welcome and not even conscious of the fact it was an established group and I was new to it because I am not usually in at that time. It was just typical of the HOSS spirit.

It was my celebration of completing my year of daily positives and the lads in the open discussion group that day made me very welcome. I wanted to be at the HOSS on the day; the following day I had a celebratory day trip to

Edinburgh on the Chieftain. I had to book a seat at a table of four for the journey back as all the single and two seater tables were taken. I was worried about how crowded it might be and what my travelling companions would be like; whether they would appreciate my being in what felt like their personal space. I took facing that fear as part of the finale to my year-long challenge. As it happened, there wasn't anyone else booked at the same table as me so I had a lovely relaxed journey; at the same time I felt I had somehow ducked out of the final part of my challenge! Very soon afterwards, though, I got on a very busy ScotRail train to Inverness and had to share a table with three people. I got into a very pleasant conversation with them about computer technology and living in the Highlands; it was fun, interesting and gave me that fitting closure. I got the best of both worlds; space and tranquility on the Chieftain and a successful challenge on my journey to Inverness and our HOSS. Blessed be!

Index

The reference may be in the numbered thought, the note following, or both. All numbers refer to the thought number, not the page on which it is found.

Telephone calls   43; 90

Travel   93; 128; 161

Unexpected changes   74; 90; 115

Working (including voluntary)   113; 126

Poems and a Short Story

Aviemore poem, November 2011

(untitled: quoted after thought number 108)

Beneath an opal sky alive
with winter's kindling energy, you catch
and bind my life to yours.
A world above in frozen fire
glows elemental; crystals locked
in latticed monument from earth to space
proclaim your voice to awe the universe.
You speak through silent alchemy;
a language all your own, where dark is light
and shines primeval brighter than the sun
with power of knowing sensuality
in silhouette. In languid curve
of resting strath encircled, you arise
and shimmer at your brightest; greet the night
in long embrace of velvet-mounted stars.
With points of shadowed evergreen,
you tap the frosted well of deepened dusk
and autograph the skyline: AVIEMORE.
You reach me through an age of patient growth
as seasons fell in years of silken waves
to build and swell my heart. You take me in;
illuminate a chain of sparkling lights
along the paths of home; define my soul.

Aviemore ski season poem, January 2012

I have never done, nor wished to do, snowsports. I freely admit I am not a sporty person; my outdoor activity tends to be restricted to low level walks and of course my enjoyment of the changing seasons. Yet somehow this poem came out of me. People who do snowsports and have had it shown to them were astonished and disbelieving when told I don't participate. It shows that autistic people can appreciate the qualities of something that is not "our thing".

The evening sky grows dark; from high
above in silent tribute down Cairngorm
a soft and constant drifting snow
of memories falls unseen to your heart.
Day upon day; fresh slopes, new skies
from dawn to dusk, adrenalin and hopes
of powder, blue and diamond rush
tomorrow; apres-ski tonight with friends.
Amid the settling sounds and warmth
you gather energy of time well spent;
each moment truly lived, so strong
they build themselves upon you, stories forged
in firelight. You keep them safe.
Electric snowflakes shine from Grampian Road;
you wear your contrasts spirited
and proud, the transient structured shift of white
on which your seasons turn displayed
throughout the night in steadfast filaments.
You greet the morning; dance with light
and dark. Within you, all begins again.

Highland Chieftain poem, December 2011

This was written when I was making plans to move to the Highlands from Edinburgh as the HOSS was being planned. I travelled on the eve of an infamous storm which caused chaos throughout Scotland. The same day the storm was due to hit, I had to attend one of the planning meetings. It was terrifying but ultimately rewarding; something I had to face and had to work hard to establish my role afterwards. Inspired on the train, I wrote the rough draft of this poem on the paper tablecloth!

Heading North, the Highland Chieftain paints
the pass at night in glittering monochrome;
in white and silver flowing through the dark
she draws a starburst wake. A blizzard turns
to finest detail spun from mountain air
as fleeting forms in bid for permanence
cling to her side with frail geometry.
She writes each moment in a flash of speed
with scores of snowflake sparks uniquely caught
and fired in moonlit calligraphic scrolls
onto the freezeframe steel of winter sky.
The scene complete, the land at rest, in calm
we travel on. She fixes me secure
in homeward rush; a guardian eye of storm,
within her focused lines is all I need
to see. The lights of Inverness arise;
electric starred horizon draws us in
and spells the future out in neon glint.

The Stereotype v Reality Autism Poems

These came from an idea in the creative writing group at the HOSS. It was suggested we write something which showed a stereotypical view of autism...

The Cliché Now Arriving...

A special interest? Why, of course!
It's trains for me; can't wait to force
them into every conversation!
Every line and every station,
each timetable learned by heart.
(Engineering works apart,
mind you; my kind can't deviate,
and God forbid them running late!)
I'll feed you engine numbers live;
a Sprinter or a 125,
I'll let you know whatever's due
and then I'll show you my tattoo!
But if you're tired or have to go,
it takes a scream to let me know,
and if you're worried, hurt or ill
or need to talk or just to chill
or mourn a loved one passed away,
I'm clueless what to do or say.
So look no deeper than the hype;
Just leave me to my stereotype.

...and then balance it out with something more representative of what autism is really like!

The Cliché Now Departing...

A special interest? Yes, intense;
I do love trains, but no offence;
you shouldn't take the joy it brings
to mean I shun all other things.
I'll talk about them, that's a fact
but don't assume I lack the tact
or will to be a friend to you
because I may just miss a cue
from time to time. I daily wake
in terror of the next mistake.
I care and feel; I listen hard
and though I may not be a bard
like all your other Facebook friends
with words to comfort when life ends
for someone loved; my "Sorry" plain
beside my picture of a train,
I will recall your favourite wine
and even if it isn't mine,
I'll bring a bottle – when you're free –
to help you smile in memory.

Three Highland Lives

A short story originally printed in the HOSS newsletter when we were based at our first premises, Albion House.

1815

On a ship leaving the Hebrides, a frightened woman, Anna holds onto a wooden post trying to make herself as small and still as possible as the rush of people and voices around her builds to a single overwhelming blur of all too much. She is leaving everything she has ever known, caught up in what will become known as the Highland Clearances; she cannot pick out a single detail of the commotion around her, yet she will remember every minute feature of that wooden pillar; the texture, the grain, the smell, until the day she dies. Her community have criticised her for not being strong and getting on with it like everyone else. She has no idea why she isn't coping like they are. Nothing makes sense. There are only questions.

2015

Standing outside Albion House with the piece of paper that answers so many questions, Adele, a newly diagnosed autistic woman watches the everyday Inverness scene with a new perspective. So that's why the wheels on the suitcase a tourist is dragging into a B&B halfway along the street sound so gratingly loud; that's why the workmen's high visibility jackets seem almost to shout at her eyes. That's why she froze when that harmless, gentle old lady asked her for directions and that's why she felt so bad about it for the rest of the week! So much makes sense now but there are still so many questions.

On the 25th floor of the controversial Tornagrain Tower, Amira, an archivist in the Brain Activity and Genealogy department, takes a break from her research to look out over the city. Sunlight glints on the glass dome of Eastgate Phase Twelve as a silver monorail train pulls in from the spaceport; further away, the River Ness sparkles between the iridescent semi-opaque six foot walls of the flood defences as crystal clear as it has run for hundreds of years. Amira cannot imagine ever leaving Inverness; she appreciates it even more for what she discovered by chance about her own family in her work on psychological traits through generations. When her remote ancestor Adele was diagnosed autistic in 2015, it was a different world; people were still learning about autism and some hadn't even heard of it. That was hard enough to imagine; Amira's friends had never needed an explanation of why she needed a quiet setting for an in depth chat yet every so often loved to lose herself in the buzz and energy of a music festival as live and loud as the Highland Chieftain's infamous bicentennial celebration in 2184. What really sent shivers down her spine was the experience of Anna, their ancestor from even further back. Nobody could have known she was autistic. Autism was completely unknown. Science doesn't yet have a full explanation of how Adele came to have a recurring dream of clinging to a wooden post on an emigrant ship; how Anna's pain, fear and bewilderment imprinted themselves on a collective unconscious to be relived through Adele's dreams as diagnosis opened her mind. Somehow it all makes sense, though there will always be questions.

Dedications

Jeni, Gill, Kirsten and Andrew: Thank you for every day.

Catherine and all at Edinburgh; Jill, Claire, Julie and all at our sister service in Perth: For ongoing trans-Druimuachdar goodwill. All hail the Highland Main Line!

Kabie and all of ARGH: For all you do and all I've learned.

Karen and Alison: Once more, 'til we three meet again.

Ann: For many happy times and inspiring late night morale boosting sessions in AvieAmazing and Nairnia.

Ruth: My go-to solidarity sounding board, everybody else's too. Taken too soon. Nos Da, fy annwyl ffrind.

Flora, Mike, Maxie, Suzi, Matilda, Mitzi, Marie, Mischa, MacMouse and my precious bundle of cattitude, Savannah Inverness: My Aviemore family, wherever I happen to live.

David and Gwen at PublishNation: For unstinting support.

My "brother" and best friend, Matthew: For sharing the best of times and pulling me through the worst of times; for deepest hilarity and highest respect. XOXO

To those whose paths have diverged professionally but with whom I share memories: Your names are still in my heart. Full inclusive acceptance remains the true goal.

To and for the Highland One Stop Shop and wider
Highland autistic community; confidentiality precludes
publishing names but big time kudos for all your courage,
empathy and solidarity.

This photograph was taken from Ness Bridge, Inverness.
For the past few years in early April our friends at ARGH
(Autism Rights Group Highland; www.arghighland.co.uk),
whose support is invaluable, have arranged for the bridge
to be lit in rainbow colours to celebrate neurodiversity.

AutismInitiatives
real partnerships, unique solutions, positive outcomes

Produced to raise funds for the Highland One
Stop Shop for autistic adults.

highlandoss.org.uk

www.autisminitiatives.org

Front cover photographs, from top: River Ness side, Inverness;
Station footbridge, Aviemore; Station entrance, Nairn (at
approximately noon and 9pm on the same day).
All taken by the author.

130

Printed in Great Britain
by Amazon